Envy

D1414821

Envy
Exposing a Secret Sin

Mary Louise Bringle

WESTMINSTER
JOHN KNOX PRESS
LOUISVILLE · KENTUCKY

First edition
Published by Westminster John Knox Press
Louisville, Kentucky

16 17 18 19 20 21 22 23 24 25—10 9 8 7 6 5 4 3 2 1

Book design by Sharon Adams
Cover design by Mark Abrams

Library of Congress Cataloging-in-Publication Data

Names: Bringle, Mary Louise.
Title: Envy : exposing a secret sin / Mary Louise Bringle.
Description: Louisville, KY : Westminster John Knox Press, 2016. | Includes index.
Identifiers: LCCN 2015034515 | ISBN 9780664259709 (alk. paper)
Subjects: LCSH: Envy--Religious aspects--Christianity.
Classification: LCC BV4627.E5 B75 2016 | DDC 241/.3--dc23 LC record available at http://lccn.loc.gov/2015034515

Most Westminster John Knox Press books are available at special quantity discounts when purchased in bulk by corporations, organizations, and special-interest groups. For more information, please e-mail SpecialSales@wjkbooks.com.

Contents

List of Figures

List of Tables

Acknowledgments

The last word in this book goes to gratitude as a key virtue to cultivate in the conquest of envy. The first word in the book fittingly goes to gratitude as well, for the many people who have been helpful over the duration of the project. I began working on envy as one of the seven deadly sins in the last millennium but was diverted from it by discovering a vocation for hymnology around the year 2000. The pages I had written on this manuscript in the 1990s might well have languished in a file cabinet drawer had not Robert Ratcliff been hired as executive editor for Westminster John Knox Press. By whatever quirk of grace, Bob had worked in an editorial capacity with Abingdon Press on two earlier books of mine related to deadly sins (*Despair: Sickness or Sin?* and *The God of Thinness: Gluttony and Other Weighty Matters*). Out of the blue, he emailed me in the spring of 2013, asking if I happened to have another sin in the pipeline . . . and I did. I can only begin to express my gratitude for his initial query and subsequent sponsorship.

Beyond this, I am grateful to Mark Stanley, pastor of Trinity Presbyterian Church in Hendersonville, North Carolina, who first suggested that I apply to the Louisville Institute for support in returning to the project. The Louisville Institute's Sabbatical Grant for Researchers Program, funded by the Religion Division of Lilly Endowment and based at Louisville Presbyterian Seminary, enables "ecclesially engaged academics" and scholarly religious leaders to conduct study intended to enrich the religious life of North American Christians. Under these auspices, I was able to take a leave of absence from Brevard College for the fall semester of 2014 to concentrate on writing new material and revising old. I am grateful to colleagues who stepped into roles I normally fill at the college to make this possible: Tom Bell and John Padgett, in particular. I am grateful to Kristina Holland, teaching colleague of many years and coordinator of the Brevard Writing Lab, who spent hours with me, meticulously checking footnotes; to Brevard College art history major Lindsey Carscaddon, who helped locate digital images, to English and philosophy major Gabrielle Smith, who assisted with indexing; and to William Throop of Green Mountain College, who provided an extensive critique of chapter 6. Remaining flaws are, of course, my own.

As always, I am grateful to Shirley Arnold, who does not have an envious bone in her body and who never complains, no matter how testy I get when writing; and to the many cats who have enlivened our household from the start of this project to its conclusion (Cinda and Elmo, Zac and Bert, Scout and Lacey): all but one of them green-eyed, but none of them monsters. Well, except at 3:00 a.m.

Mary Louise Bringle

Introduction: Eating Our Hearts Out

Of all the seven deadly sins, envy alone involves no pleasure.[1] Greed delights in possessions; gluttony, in food and drink; and lust, in sex. Pride revels in its sense of superiority; anger, in its outrage at being wronged and its schemes for punishing wrongdoers. Even sloth, if it can be bothered, derives some small gratification from doing little and aiming low.

Granted, a measure of perverse enjoyment may sneak through the back door of envy in the related emotion of Schadenfreude, the petty spite that finds pleasure in another person's distress. But in its front door manifestation, feeling outclassed that someone else has or has accomplished something we have not, envy is no fun at all. The Roman poet Horace claimed that even the tyrants of Sicily could devise no more painful torment than envy—and these were the inventive geniuses who came up with the "brazen bull" as an execution chamber: a life-sized bronze statue inside which condemned persons were locked as fires were set underneath, roasting the poor souls to death while converting their screams into sounds like the animal's bellowing.

If envy is even worse torment than this, why would anyone choose to write (or, for that matter, read) a book about it? The answer, I think, is fairly simple. Insofar as most of us want happiness in our lives, not only for ourselves but also for others, we stand to benefit from learning about the habits that promote human flourishing—and, though less pleasantly, the ones that get in the way. Centuries ago, the tradition of Christian moral theology came up with the rubric of the *seven deadly sins* and their contrasting virtues as a framework for analyzing such habits. Since graduate school, I have been fascinated by mining the riches of this tradition for thinking about challenges to human flourishing in the present.

For the first two deadly sins I submitted to examination, my interest was easier to explain to other people. When I was working on despair—an affiliate of the sin of sloth—colleagues with whom I talked about the project would often say something along the lines of: "Oh, would you like to interview me?" When I was examining gluttony in relation to the current epidemic of eating disorders, women in particular would prick up their ears. As I was writing on these earlier projects, I could keep myself motivated by imagining a person who might venture to a bookstore looking for some resource to help in sifting through personal and theological issues related to depression or diet.

It seems unlikely, though, that anyone would approach the salesperson at such a bookstore with the query, "Say, do you have anything good on *envy*?" But to my mind, the very unlikelihood of the question suggests a problem worth diagnosing. On the one hand, we in the early twenty-first century in the United States are surrounded by a commercial culture that no longer views public envy as a serious concern—indeed, that readily uses provocation to envy as a marketing ploy. On the other hand, we remain sufficiently embarrassed by our own private bouts with this under-analyzed experience that we are minimally apt to own up to it. After all, if I honestly admit that I am envious of a friend's success, I as much as concede not only my sense of inferiority but also the pettiness of my begrudging spirit. Who would want to do that? Envy thus remains for many of us a secret sin, and it festers in its secrecy.

Such festering gives us all the more reason to draw envy out of the closet, exposing it to the clear light of day. Many of us can surely acknowledge being disturbed by the ugly extremes to which competitiveness-gone-astray drives certain members of our society: financial speculators, compulsive dieters, overly zealous parents at their children's Little League games. The Winter Olympics in 2014 even took time revisiting, twenty years after the fact, the infamous Tonya Harding/Nancy Kerrigan knee-whack scandal of the 1990s. Thinking somewhat closer to home, we can also acknowledge chagrin at the seemingly chronic dissatisfaction of some of our youth: the malaise among those in affluent circumstances at "having it all and wanting more" (the title of a research paper on global wealth and poverty, published in January 2015 by Oxfam International); the willingness among some in less affluent circumstances to kill another child over nothing more meaningful than a pair of designer running shoes. Closest of all: if we let our eyes become educated to the multiple guises in which envy masquerades, we begin to see how our own happiness gets soured by feelings of resentment, hankering after what we do not have rather than cherishing what we do.

Such hankering takes multiple forms. The decade of the 1980s in the United States, for example, came to be known in some circles as the "age of greed." Shortly thereafter, one commentator proposed labeling the 1990s the "age of envy."[2] The label never stuck, but there were good reasons behind the proposal—reasons that have, if anything, grown increasingly pertinent over the intervening years. First Baby Boomers and then Generation Xers, both groups reared under relative prosperity, began reaching midlife—and with it, a sobering encounter with nonnegotiable limits. A person who chose not to pursue a certain career path now found it too late to pursue; another who put off having children came to realize that the opportunity had sadly passed. As the health of aging parents began failing, we came to realize that age and ill health would inevitably catch up with us, too. Fluctuating economic challenges through the first decades of the twenty-first century brought on waves of furloughs and "downsizing"—renamed "right-sizing" in an attempt to make it more palatable—and widespread job insecurity. The Generation Y "Millennials," whom I now teach, face a daunting job market after graduation from college and often do so saddled with crushing debt from loans taken out to finance their education. Is it any wonder, then, that we might nurse bitter feelings over things other people seem to enjoy that we do not? In her insightful analysis of the deadly sins as "glittering vices," Rebecca Konyndyk DeYoung uses precisely this language to sum up envy: it is "feeling bitter when others have it better."[3]

Beyond these generational factors, conversation about envy appears particularly timely for a further reason. Every once in a while, the seven deadly sins make a comeback as a topic for discussion—as well as subject matter for tattoos, T-shirts, and the titles of romance novels. From 2003 to 2006, for example, the New York Public Library Lectures in the Humanities published a series of small books on each of the "deadlies," following in the footsteps of a comparable collection of *London Sunday Times* op-ed pieces from the 1960s. Also around the turn of the twenty-first century, philosopher Robert Solomon compiled a series of essays on the sins under the title *Wicked Pleasures* and humorist Dan Savage undertook to commit each of the sins himself and write about his experiences in *Skipping towards Gomorrah*.[4] But the titles of the last two works in particular are revealing. In them, as in many of the other popular press renditions, the word "sin" is used with a bit of a sneer, as if the concept itself were old-fashioned and repressive, a prudish attempt by finger-wagging moralists to keep people from having fun.

In some ways, those of us who consider ourselves to be religious people bring this misinterpretation upon ourselves. As early as the 1940s, Dorothy Sayers gave an address to the Moral Welfare Society of the Church of England titled "The Other Six Deadly Sins."[5] It takes little imagination to get her point. Public religious talk about "sin"—perhaps even more now than in Sayers's day—seems to focus almost exclusively on sex. As happened in the nineteenth century over the issue of slavery, so in the twenty-first, entire denominations are splitting over differing interpretations of a few biblical passages: this time, passages about sexual practices gleaned from scriptural vice lists. But, regardless of how these sexual prohibitions are interpreted, New Testament vice lists are perfectly clear in condemning evil intentions from the human heart (Mark 7:21–23), works of the flesh that contrast with the fruit of the Spirit (Gal. 5:19–21), and the corruption that comes from ceasing to honor and acknowledge God (Rom. 1:24–31). *Envy* figures in all these lists and deserves at least as much attention from moralists as any sexual practice.

The following chapters supply such attention. Chapter 1, "Envy Appeal," argues that envy has been "de-moralized" over the past 150 years in the United States as a result of the combined triumphs of the commercial (the rise of advertising) and the therapeutic (the emergence of "feel-good" psychologies). Thus, even though we may still be embarrassed to admit to the feelings of inferiority that motivate our envy of others' successes, we no longer experience any *ethical qualms* about such feelings. Chapter 2, "Rival Definitions," works to clarify the ill-understood meaning of the word "envy" itself, exploring the array of invidious passions that were incorporated under the heading of Capital Envy by the deadly sins tradition and then differentiating "envy proper" from related affective states: jealousy, resentment, covetousness, spite, indignation, and Schadenfreude (malicious glee).

Many members of the audience initially targeted by the deadly sins tradition were not literate—a fact that parallels in interesting ways our own "post-literate" (or at least, fast-becoming "post-print") culture. For such audiences, pictures and stories communicate far more effectively than discursive prose. Thus, chapter 3, "Arresting Images," explores the ways medieval and Renaissance artists portrayed envy in illuminated manuscripts, frescoes, wood prints, and engravings. In their original day, these images exerted cautionary force. In our own, they still lurk in the background of common figures of speech: "Eat your heart out" (significantly transformed in our day into a taunt directed at our neighbors, whereas originally it was a description of the self-destructive activity of eating our own hearts); "I'd like to be in his shoes"; "It's a dog-eat-dog world." Chapter 4, "Telling Tales," revisits the stories that once shaped—and might well shape again—our understanding of the deep costs of envious behaviors: from Aesop and Aeschylus, through Dante and Spenser, up to Marlowe's Dr. Faust.

Beginning with fairy tales, another genre of culturally shaping stories, chapter 5, "Spoiled Psyches," examines ways both popular and academic psychology help us understand the dynamics of rivalry and also questions whether envy is an inevitable part of the struggle for survival (as evolutionary psychologists would have us believe). Chapter 6, "Polis Envy," acknowledges attempts by some recent analysts to re-moralize envy by naming it as the motivation in a so-called "politics of envy" involved in attempts to bridge income inequalities. Assessing this use of the "envy" label returns to a distinction, broached in chapter 2, between legitimate yearnings for justice and illegitimate begrudging the successes of others.

Ultimately, though, the point of writing about envy moves beyond diagnosis to proposals for healing—the focus for chapter 7, "Redeeming Virtues." Just as the word "sin" needs to be rehabilitated from a near-obsessive sexual focus, so the word "virtue" also needs reclaiming. Rather than finger-pointing priggishness, virtuous living embodies attitudes and practices that help us flourish as individuals and communities. Spiritual directors of the deadly sins tradition gave suggestions for such habits. Stories of modern-day moral exemplars do so as well, inviting us to rethink our relationships with ourselves, our neighbors, our material environment, and our ultimate context. Once we expose the secret sin of envy to the light, we can begin to cultivate in its place an array of new habits: humility, generosity, simplicity, and gratitude. Such habits not only help us escape from the miseries of envy but, more than this, fill our formerly soured and self-devoured hearts with increasingly abundant living.

Chapter One

Envy Appeal

On January 30, 1991, swarms of journalists descended upon the once-quiet town of Channelview, Texas. Reputable newspapers and tabloids alike blazed with headlines proclaiming a bizarre "Texas Cheerleader Murder" investigation. Technically, the title was inaccurate: no murder had been committed, of a cheerleader or anyone else. Even so, the details of the case were sordid enough to spark frenzied attention.[1]

The key figure in the case was a woman named Wanda Holloway. The product of a strict, fundamentalist upbringing, Wanda lived for and through her children—particularly her daughter Shanna. Wanda had not been allowed to be a cheerleader when she was growing up, because her father thought the team's outfits were too sexually provocative. Perhaps a result, she channeled her thwarted ambitions into her daughter's career.

The trouble began in Shanna's elementary school years. She became friends with a girl her age who lived nearby: Amber Heath. When Wanda was supporting her children as a single mother by commuting to a job in nearby Houston, Shanna often went home after school with Amber so that Amber's mother, Verna, could keep a watchful eye over them both. While Wanda may have been grateful for this child-care arrangement, she also endured the stress of always being on the receiving end of a relationship. Such inequalities can prove a fertile breeding ground for resentment and envy.

The first evidence of bitter feelings emerged during a gymnastics class in which both Shanna and Amber were enrolled at Channelview Christian Academy. Amber, who had been twirling a baton and practicing acrobatic moves since she was two, easily became the star. At a closing performance for parents, she danced away with the greatest applause. Shanna

1

may have felt some envy at the accomplishments of her friend; after all, an eleven-year-old's self-esteem might understandably be shaken by a rival's superiority. What is less understandable is the reaction of Shanna's mother. Rather than help Shanna develop ways of coping with a world in which people are blessed with unequal gifts, Wanda became accusatory. She blamed the gymnastics teachers for showing favoritism toward Amber and began piecing together an explanatory framework by which Amber and her mother stood as chief obstacles to her daughter's—and her own—happiness.

This framework solidified in subsequent years. In seventh-grade cheerleader tryouts, Amber again emerged victorious, making the squad while Shanna did not. In fact, numerous other girls had participated in the tryouts, some successfully and some unsuccessfully, but these others did not enter into Wanda Holloway's calculations. In her view, Shanna lost only because Amber had *taken* the slot Shanna deserved.

Wanda Holloway would not let her daughter be so thwarted. With eighth-grade tryouts just a year ahead, she launched into high gear. She had a studio constructed in the garage to the Holloway house. She hired an instructor to supervise Shanna's workouts. She set up a schedule of daily practice sessions that were to take precedence over everything else in her daughter's life, including homework. Not content to rest her confidence in Shanna's developing talents, Wanda also began politicking at the junior high, a step that was to prove her undoing.

Since cheerleaders were chosen by vote of the student body, rules for the competition prohibited contestants from distributing favors to buy the allegiance of their classmates. Wanda Holloway later claimed that the school enacted this rule at the last minute, without her knowledge. But however the rule came into being, the other girls in the cheerleading competition abided by it. At her mother's insistence, Shanna did not. Wanda had her daughter's name printed on hundreds of rulers to give to all her classmates. This act violated the terms of the competition and Shanna was disqualified.

Wanda was enraged. She wept hysterically in the principal's office when she was informed of the decision. Shanna simply asked if she could get back to her classes and get on with her day. Meanwhile Wanda seethed . . . and began plotting her revenge.

The envy in this unfolding psychodrama now clearly belonged *not* to fourteen-year-old Shanna but to thirty-seven-year-old Wanda Holloway—envy of Amber Heath, the successful cheerleader, and of Verna Heath, the successful cheerleader's mother. For years Wanda had felt "one-down" in her relationship with the Heaths. As a result of this latest humiliation, she felt even lower. Unable to tolerate the contrast between her rivals' supposed happiness and her own misery, she began looking for ways to even the score.

Thus far in the story, it is not overly difficult to identify with Wanda Holloway's feelings. Even if we object to her attempts to stage-manage her daughter's life, we can feel some sympathy for a woman who had felt deprived of opportunities for affirmation in her life and was hungry for success. In Channelview, Texas, one conventional route to success for women was cheerleading. While our contexts may differ, most of us can identify with the pain of feeling diminished by the success of a rival. We do not applaud the sentiments, but we can grasp the desire to "get even."

Where we likely part company with Wanda Holloway is in the lengths to which we would be willing to go to even the score with a rival. In the most sordid twist of the "Texas Cheerleader Case," Wanda Holloway conspired to have her rivals murdered.

The proceedings of this conspiracy are all on tape; otherwise, they would be too outlandish to be believed. Wanda Holloway contacted Terry Harper, noted local ne'er-do-well and brother of her first husband, thinking that his checkered past might give him access to people who could be hired for a contract killing. Harper was at first incredulous and then fearful that his prior misdemeanor convictions might land him in bigger trouble if Wanda really followed through on her plans. He decided to report what he knew to the local sheriff's office, and law enforcement officials wired him for his subsequent meetings with her.

The conversations recorded from those meetings reveal a woman whose thought processes had been completely twisted by envy. The rivalry that *she* felt toward Verna and Amber Heath was translated into *their* presumed efforts to make her and her daughter miserable. *They* were meddling with Shanna's chances to make the cheerleading squad, getting Shanna disqualified from the competition. *They* were making Wanda sick to her stomach—they, and not the envy eating away at her insides.

But by far the most appalling feature of the conversations recorded on the sheriff department's surveillance tapes was Wanda's apparent glee at the prospect of doing away with her rivals. In the initial phone tap, Harper asked her, "You still interested in taking care of that problem?" "Uh huhh! Yeah!" she exclaimed, giggling with unmistakable enthusiasm. Her only qualm was the potential expense involved. When she hesitated, he gave her an out: "Now, if you don't want to do it, I'll understand . . ." "Well," she protested, "it's not that I don't wanna do it. I just gotta get the money."

Finally, she decided to limit her requested "hits" to Verna alone. "The mother's the one that's doing all the damage," she reasoned—still oblivious to the fact that any "damage" being done was in her own head. "I should go with the mother. And the kid, maybe she'd be screwed with the mother. Maybe it would mess with her mind."

At one brief moment in the surveillance tapes, Wanda Holloway seemed about to come to her senses. "I get so mad at things," she confessed. "I think, 'I could just shoot you.' I don't think I could ever do that." Fair enough. No doubt many of us have been prey to moments of blinding rage when we wished destruction on our adversaries; but then, we have recognized the danger of those feelings and repented of them. Not so, Wanda Holloway. In the very next breath, she said to Harper, "This is the only way I could do it . . . is pay somebody." She laughed— nervous, giddy laughter. Then, "OK!" she exclaimed. And, almost like the cheerleader she never got to be, "Let's go for it!!"

Fortunately, no "Texas cheerleader murder"—or Texas cheerleader's mother's murder—ever took place. Terry Harper turned over the surveillance tapes, and the $2,500 diamond earrings that Wanda had given him as payment for a potential "hit man," to the Harris County organized crimes task force. Wanda Holloway was arrested on charges of conspiracy to commit murder. When the case went to trial, national and international news media were present to cover the story. While banned from the courtroom for the balance of the proceedings, reporters and cameras were admitted to the closing arguments. Chief Prosecutor Mike Anderson summed up the emotional drama of the defendant's imagined rivalry with the Heaths: "It gnawed at her day and night," he concluded. "It gnawed at her to the point of obsession." Indeed it did. If there was one victim more grievously injured than all the others by this consumptive envy, it was Wanda Holloway herself.

When this frustrated, eager woman finally found the spotlight that had been denied her all her life, it was the unflattering one of national scandal. Even years after her trial, the misnamed "Texas Cheerleader Murder Case" provided the focus of an episode in the A&E network's *American Justice* series and two made-for-television movies. We continue to be fascinated with the Wanda Holloway story because it projects into bright relief some of the darker imaginings of our own hearts: the yearning for fulfillments that seem cruelly withheld; the sting of defeat and resultant sense of personal belittlement; the resentful search for people to blame for our misfortune; the hunger to take our rivals down a notch, by whatever means; the relish at savoring their potential "comeuppance." According to classical definitions, envy involves both sadness at another's good fortune and happiness at another's ill fortune; envy lurks in both grudge-bearing misery and malicious glee. Wanda Holloway's story offers a case study in both dimensions. While her distorted thoughts, feelings, and actions may differ from ours in *degree*, they do not differ altogether in *kind*.

Of course, the difference in degree matters. Wanda Holloway received a six-month term in jail as "shock probation" for her envy-motivated actions. My own occasional envious fantasies earn me only the prison sentence of my own tortured mind. In either case, however—Wanda's or my own—the perversity of the experiences raises questions. What in our *nature* prompts us to indulge such vicious responses to our assumed competitors? What in our *culture* makes it even *thinkable* for an individual to hand over $2,500 in an effort to get someone killed—and for nothing more than a cheerleading rivalry? While we will need the balance of this book to respond to such queries, in what remains of this chapter I want to look directly at the second, suggesting two major factors in our culture's complicity with envy gone overboard: the triumph of the commercial and the triumph of the therapeutic.

The Triumph of the Commercial

Over the past century in the United States, attitudes toward envy have shifted. Like the subject of a before-and-after feature story, envy has undergone a makeover to camouflage its sickly greenish cast. Once a deadly sin and focus for moralists' warnings, it has lately become a centerpiece for marketers' hype: "Buy this product and you will be the *envy* of all your friends!" As if envy itself were morally neutral, and provocation to envy, all done in the spirit of good, clean, competitive fun.

But envy is *not* morally neutral, as the Texas Cheerleader Murder case reveals. Envy corrodes our spirits, gnawing away at our hearts from the inside. Once we let the cattiness out of the bag, so to speak, its claws can wreak havoc of unanticipated proportions: murder and conspiracy to commit murder, vandalism, character assassination. Those of us who live in the early twenty-first century in the United States need to recognize that we consign envy to secrecy—shielding our eyes from its moral dangers—to our significant peril. The emergence of consumer culture is key in contributing to this shielding process.

The big shift from an economy of production to an economy of consumption in this country occurred during the latter half of the nineteenth century. From roughly 1865 to 1920, a predominantly rural-farming economy gave way to an urban-manufacturing one. Large-scale factories and the potential for mass production increased the availability of goods for sale. At the same time, cheap and dependable land transportation, including the recently completed transcontinental railroad, made these goods available to broader and broader markets. An increase in earnings meant that even working-class families began to enjoy some discretionary income. Improved literacy combined with heightened geographic and social mobility enabled unprecedented numbers of people to aspire to middle-class status.

The earlier preindustrial economy had functioned hand-to-mouth, as supply was barely able to keep pace with demand. The new manufacturing economy, by contrast, functioned more "hand-to-pocket": able for the first time in history to produce more merchandise than existing demand could accommodate, it faced the novel challenge of *creating* demand, generating a cohort of consumers eager to reach for their wallets to buy up the surplus. A newly configured advertising industry rose to meet this challenge.

As late as 1870, economic historian James Norris notes, magazines like the popular *Harper's* carried very few advertisements, and these were confined to a separate section at the back of the publication. Most of the promoted goods were essentials rather than luxury items. Advertisers focused their appeal on practical matters of usefulness, craftsmanship, and value—matters having to do with nature of the *object* itself and not with the character of its prospective *consumer*.[2]

This focus began to change in the last decades of the nineteenth century. With disposable income on the rise and an abundance of mass-produced goods available, copywriters discovered they could promote some of these goods as status markers, indicators that their purchasers had scaled the ladder of success. By 1899, Thorstein Veblen had coined the term "conspicuous consumption" to describe the dynamic by which a society without inherited social classes substituted *purchasing power* to mark social and economic rank.[3]

The focus of advertising copy thus shifted from the object to the consumer, from assurances of practicality to promises of intangibles like social status. Even items that once had been seen as purely utilitarian—soap, for example—changed their pitch from the purity of the product to the attractiveness of the user. In such a context, it did not take long

Figure 1. The Palmolive Company, item ID BH1000, used by permission from the Ad*Access Digital Collection of the John W. Hartman Center for Sales, Advertising, and Marketing History at Duke University.

for the appeal to interpersonal comparisons to grow explicit. A 1922 ad for Palmolive soap, for example, encouraged women to cultivate the skin "women envy and men admire." (See Figure 1.)

A comic strip drawn by A. R. Momand during the decades from 1913 to 1931 provided a title for the ensuing race to keep pace in the status game: "Keeping Up with the Joneses."[4] Cultural and social historian Susan Matt has taken this idiom as the title for a book in which she uses memoirs, magazine articles, sermons, and sociological studies to identify the decades from 1890 to 1930 as the period in U.S. history when the voices of moralists urging us to keep a tight rein on envy gave way to the voices of secular commentators urging it instead as a spur for economic growth.[5]

"Keeping up"—or better yet, getting ahead—became an especially potent motif in advertisements for luxury items. Automobiles led the way. One of the first forthright "envy" appeals made its appearance in a Cadillac ad that ran in a 1915 edition of the *Saturday Evening Post*. Interestingly enough, not a single feature of the automobile being promoted appeared in the copy. Instead, that copy focused on a so-called "Penalty of Leadership":

> Whether . . . leadership be vested in a man or in a manufactured product, emulation and envy are ever at work. . . . When a man's work becomes a standard for the whole world, it also becomes a target for the shafts of the envious few.[6]

The ad thus suggested that people who purchased Cadillacs would, by that very act, be demonstrating how they were intimidated neither by work of exceptional quality nor by the prospect of receiving "shafts of envy" from their less-discerning neighbors.

When the new field of telecommunications took hold at midcentury, it followed Cadillac's precedent. In 1952, a magazine ad for a "teleset"—a cabinet combining a television and record player—warned prospective buyers that they should "expect to be envied." The ad continued, smugly: "That's part of getting a DuMont."[7] In short, provoking one's neighbors was no longer perceived as a cost; it was an outright *benefit* of success.

While the envy-appeal in marketing grew in the middle decades of the twentieth century, its fuller flowering awaited the century's close. The decades of the 1960s and '70s had hailed the advent of an anti-consumerist "Age of Aquarius," but the '80s brought with them a new set of economic insecurities and with them, according to analyst Laurence Shames, a new kind of status anxiety. People in the middle class began struggling to preserve the appearance that they were not sliding backward. To this end, status symbols made a comeback. Shames concludes: "'Sensibility' eighties-style . . . had less to do with connoisseurship"—with appreciating the excellent craft of items like Cadillac automobiles or DuMont telesets—than with "knowing which stuff was the right stuff, which stuff would be recognized, approved, and *envied*."[8]

Where once envy had been a deadly sin to be cautioned against, as we will see in future chapters, now it was a commercial property to be exploited. At the turn of the twenty-first century, more and more pro-moters jumped on the no-longer-banned wagon. Automobiles again led the way: "Now there's another [BMW] M3 to cherish (or envy)," read a promotional article in *AutoWeek*.[9] An ad for the 2001 Jaguar XK8 went even further. As a camera zoomed in on the car's various features, names of the seven deadly sins appeared on the screen. Preceded by a flash of green, "Envy" accompanied a shot of the luxurious interior.[10] One reviewer demonstrated that he grasped the underlying point of the campaign. Practicality and cost are not the point, he wrote: "What counts is whether other people eye you with envy; whether the car gets respect from the valet at snooty restaurants. Will it get parked out front? Or does it go around back with all the others?"[11]

For luxury in a lower price bracket than automobiles, digital electron-ics followed the marketing trail earlier blazed by "telesets." Scanners and pagers were among the items promoted as ways to provoke envy from friends and coworkers. Within the first two decades of the twenty-first century, "Envy" had even come to be an explicit product name, with Hewlett Packard's debut of a line of Envy computers. In 2006 Verizon and LG jointly heralded their "enV" (pronounced "envy") models as "the envy of all mobile phones."[12] Not to be outdone, in 2013 AT&T intro-duced its "Next" plan, whereby customers could regularly trade in their current phones when newer models came along. The advertising spot for this program began with the telling lines: "We love our devices . . . until we see the new one," followed by images of people ignoring their own gadgets while craning their necks to view their neighbors' presumably more current and coveted versions.[13]

Meanwhile, following in the path of Palmolive soap, other cosmetic items joined the ranks of envy-promoting products. In March of 1997, Gucci launched a fragrance named "Gucci Envy." Seven years later, it followed with "Gucci Envy Me," marketed explicitly as "a fragrance for the egocentric and bold young woman."[14] Meanwhile, for health-and-beauty-conscious individuals wanting services and not just products, Envy Medical, Inc., emerged in the 2010s as "one of the most exciting medical technology companies . . . in the field of dermatology and medi-cal aesthetics," while Massage Envy Spas began sprouting up around the country, offering less clinical care options from facials to foot scrubs.[15]

What is going on here? To put matters into perspective: can we imag-ine driving a car marketed as "Road Rage," proudly toting a laptop named "Arrogance," or dabbing on an enticing bit of "Spite" perfume? Yet, we seem to think nothing of doing the equivalent with products sporting an "Envy" label.

This makeover of a once-deadly sin into a major marketing appeal comes with hidden costs. Individually, we pay out of our self-confidence and contentment. Whether we are the envied ones or the enviers, we find ourselves perpetually checking our mirrors: to see if we measure up to the established norms of status; to see if our neighbors are gaining on or outstripping us. Even our capacity to enjoy what we do have gets short-circuited by our eagerness to make sure our rivals know that we have it, and our fear that they may in fact have *more* or *better* of it—whatever "it" is—than we do. Thus, as Christopher Lasch remarked years ago about our "culture of narcissism," the "propaganda of consumption" creates "new forms of unhappiness," generating questions like these: "Do you look dowdy next to your neighbors? Do you own a car inferior to theirs? Are your children as healthy? As popular?" He concluded: "Advertising institutionalizes envy and its attendant anxieties."[16]

But the hidden price tag of the envy-appeal in advertising goes beyond individual insecurity and discontent. We pay socially as well. Envy-fueled economies are geared toward constant growth, not sustainability. What may have "worked" in a period of industrial expansion in the early twentieth century makes less sense in a twenty-first-century context newly aware of limited environmental resources. The rush to replace barely used consumer goods or to "keep up with the Joneses" by purchasing more and more luxury items creates extravagant waste and poses heavy ecological costs.

Further, what happens to interpersonal relationships in a climate of constant comparisons? If envy is of such little consequence that it can be used, with a wink and a knowing smile, to promote goods from soap to spa treatments, why should we feel moral misgivings about envying our neighbor's success—in a cheerleading competition or any other arena? In an extensive review of scholarly reflections on the consequences of advertising, Richard W. Pollay, curator of the History of Advertising Archives at the University of British Columbia, has determined that ads promoting social rivalry bring in their wake the loss of cooperation, charity, and compassion. He sadly concludes: "Relations with neighbors, the proverbial Joneses we strive to keep up with, are increasingly based on envy, emulation, and competition. . . . But social competition can turn asocial and precipitate violence and theft."[17] The *triumph of the commercial* leads to the conquest of the communal. Just ask Verna Heath and Wanda Holloway.

The Triumph of the Therapeutic

The triumph of the commercial, however, has not occurred in a vacuum. At the same time as advertising copy writers began playing on status anxieties to fuel consumption, the old institutions that once fostered moral education—church and synagogue, school and family—were falling into disrepair. As early as the turn of the twentieth century in this country, Richard Fox and T. J. Jackson Lears explain, "The old religious sanctions for moral life, a life of sacrifice and toil, had begun to disintegrate in the face of both Darwin and the liberalization of Protestantism itself."[18] Supernatural beliefs waned and ethical convictions waffled. As they did so, old goals of transcendence and hopes for ultimate satisfaction after death gave way to new ideals of self-fulfillment and immediate gratification.

Critic Philip Rieff has summarized this value transition as "the triumph of the therapeutic."[19] According to his analysis, a new human ideal arrived on the scene in the twentieth century. Eager to escape from a repressive culture of self-denial, these new "psychological" humans turned from religious authorities to other types of guides—frequently, therapists—for assistance in achieving personal fulfillment. Tellingly for our purposes, Rieff noted a sharp conflict between the emergent gospel of fulfillment and earlier talk of "sin," which lost much of its power. Feelings of guilt ceased being experienced as calls for repentance and instead became signals of maladjustment.

Others besides Rieff have chronicled the history of a therapeutic culture in the United States.[20] Most analysts lay the credit—or blame—at the feet of liberal Protestantism. Intellectually, attempts to cope with the challenges posed by Darwinian evolution led to a loosening of biblical literalism and, with it, a general questioning of former absolutes. Meanwhile, socially, the shift from a rural-agrarian to an urban-industrial economy was loosening ties to things like home and family and the land. Lears highlights the growth of a new professional-managerial class of employees in the service sector of the economy in late-nineteenth-century America—not coincidentally, those at whom the first envy-appeals in marketing were targeted. Members of this new class felt cut off from the "real life" they had earlier known: eating food out of cans instead of fresh off the farm, living with central heating rather than natural changes of season, getting up and going to bed according to the demands of the work day rather than the rhythms of the sun. Alienated, anonymous, adrift without any sense of connection to once-familiar values, many members of this urban bourgeoisie fell victim to what came to be called "neurasthenia," a form of debilitating depression.

Hoping to address this malaise, Protestant clergy forged an alliance with the new science of psychology coming out of European sources like Sigmund Freud but also out of homegrown authorities like G. Stanley Hall. In addition to conducting research in educational psychology, Hall wrote extensively of the need to revitalize the languishing late-Victorian culture. In *Jesus Christ, in the Light of Psychology* (1917), he portrayed Jesus as an inspiring, vigorous, zestful hero figure—quite the opposite of a late-nineteenth or early-twentieth-century neurasthenic. In *Morale: The Supreme Standard of Life and Conduct* (1920), he called for the development of a human ideal focused on exuberance and vitality, celebrating the "kingdom of God" as abundant life *here and now*.

A kindred spirit, Harry Emerson Fosdick also participated in the alliance of Christianity with the emerging culture of therapy. Perhaps the most influential preacher of his day, Fosdick, like Hall, painted the picture of a physically energetic Jesus as the role model for an *Adventurous Religion* (1926) that would lead its practitioners to "radiant and triumphant living."[21] Fosdick's disciples carried such triumphalist teachings to extremes. The more they celebrated "natural" and "instinctual" human potentials as good, the more they set aside talk of "sin" and "morality" as repressive and unhelpful. Lears concludes: "Convinced that they were using psychology to renew spirituality, [liberal Protestant ministers] hastened the drift toward a more secular society." Talk about the "psyche" displaced concern for the "soul." Even more pointedly, in this new religious culture in which the therapeutic had triumphed, *morale* came to matter more than *morality*.[22]

As a culture of consumption has thus taken the place of a culture of confession and repentance, we have found ourselves increasingly stimulated to envy by advertisers' appeals yet deprived of appropriate means for dealing with the emotions that result. To say that envy has been "de-moralized" in our culture is not, therefore, to say that it has been disarmed. It still hurts; we are still abashed to have to admit to ourselves, much worse to others, that we experience this secret sin. But our discomfort is no longer a *moral shame* over failing to love our neighbors as ourselves. Rather, it is a *psychological embarrassment* over the implications of personal impotence and inferiority that come from admitting someone else has gotten sufficiently "up" on us to disturb our self-image. Envy troubles us, not because it is an indication of malice or pettiness or perversity of the will, but because it signals that greatest failing of all for believers in the gospel of self-fulfillment: namely, low self-esteem.

We should be clear. Much in the therapeutic analysis of and response to envy appears both wise and right. In terms of strategy, expressing compassionate concern seems preferable to engaging in finger-pointing condemnation. In terms of substance, focusing on envy's emergence out of a bruised and fragile ego seems key. It is not so much *what* the therapists say that is troubling but rather the framework within which they say it—and what is left *unsaid* as a result. The therapeutic framework lacks any societal perspective that notes how envy eats away at compassion while promoting lifestyles that are ecologically as well as interpersonally unsustainable. It also lacks any transcendent perspective attuned to sources beyond the self and the ways in which gratitude toward these sources supplants the need for envious comparisons. Without such larger perspectives (which we will explore in our closing chapter), therapeutic counsel promises little toward a deep transformation of character or culture. At best, it offers an array of preliminary techniques for coping with an unpleasant emotion.

Psychiatrist Robert Coles is perhaps the best of the therapeutic authors on envy to publish in the popular press.[23] He has written a telling article about a client, a young lawyer, who kept trying to unearth reasons for his restlessness, anxiety, and insomnia—and in particular, for a kind of steadily humming hostility that he felt toward the other lawyers who worked at his firm. After weeks of frustrating explorations, Coles began one afternoon—almost randomly—to fill in a lengthening silence by remarking on rivalrous thoughts about colleagues of his own that occasionally went through his mind. When he paused for a moment, he became aware of the fact that the quality of silence in the room had thickened. He looked over at his client and discovered that he was in tears.

"How deeply ashamed of himself [this client] felt as he began to speak of envy," Coles writes: envy of the fancy colleges his colleagues had attended, in contrast to the small school at which he had studied; of the fancy colleges his colleagues' *wives* had attended, when his own wife did not even have a college degree; of the moneyed family backgrounds and extravagant vacations that were topics of his colleagues' water-cooler conversations, in response to which the client himself felt so "outclassed." Coles writes with the utmost of sympathy for his client—indeed, for all of us who struggle with such feelings of humiliating inadequacy. His candor and concern are moving. But something in his analysis stops short.

He includes an interesting throwaway line toward the end of the article. He writes: "One afternoon, my lawyer friend wondered aloud at great length about envy: How common is it, and is it 'wrong—oh, excuse me—is it abnormal?'" In that very rephrasing of the question, from "wrong" to "abnormal," we recognize the triumph of the therapeutic. Moral judgments are no longer in keeping; we simply want to know that we are not significantly different from everyone else. Coles's response is to assure the client of his normalcy. "Envy is part of our humanity," he consoles; "and if envy brings the pain of knowing what we lack, envy can also lead us to reflection." Under the duress of envy, we learn to ask ourselves "who we really are, and what we really want out of life."

In Coles's response, we may hear resonances of liberal Protestant calls for vibrant, self-directed living. What we do *not* hear, however, is any further discussion of ways in which envy really might be "wrong." After all, even if it *is* "part of our humanity," so are many other things—aggression, for example—which we nevertheless feel called to keep in check. What we do not hear in Coles, after the important initial empathy, is any attempt to note the potential impact of his client's envious feelings on the welfare of his *community*. How does his admitted hostility affect the working conditions of his colleagues? How does his acknowledged embarrassment about his wife's education level affect *her* or their marital relationship? From a perspective on envy that has not been thoroughly "de-moralized" by the triumph of the therapeutic, such community-oriented questions uncover potential injuries to be repented of and rectified, altogether apart from the wounds of the self that need to be salved. In other words, matters of morality—and not merely of morale—are at stake.

Moreover, from a moralist's perspective, the envy Coles's client confesses does not simply testify to a bruised and fragile ego in need of shoring up. Paradoxically, it also professes to an inflated ego in need of humbling. Appropriate timing is critical, and to move to such humbling too quickly would clearly invite a pastoral or therapeutic disaster. But at some point, do we not need to confront the outright *ingratitude* that leaves us pining away after the successes of others while disregarding our own blessings? Even if we are so secular as to think of ourselves as self-made people, we still owe a debt of appreciation to the contexts and communities that have contributed to our making: the limbs and faculties that facilitate our daily functioning; the gifts and opportunities that have helped us on our way; the people who have supported or cared for or challenged us. What a metaphorical slap in the face it is to all these benefits to keep enviously wishing we could be in someone else's place instead. How much more of an appreciative, humbling debt do we owe if our orienting framework acknowledges a sacred mystery that surrounds our living, out of which we emerge and to which return, from whose graces our very being is a gift? The triumph of the therapeutic minimizes this mystery. The loss is significant. Not only, therefore, has our envying been "de-moralized." When not held to account to something greater than ourselves, *we* become de-moralized and diminished as well.

Coles is, however, much better than other exemplars of the therapeutic response to envy. His probing observations about the way envy can cause us to reflect on what we really do want out of our living seem soberly judicious in contrast to the more vulgarized pop culture treatments of the emotion. For example: an article in *Cosmopolitan*, entitled "Envy: Is It Hurting or (Surprise) Helping You?"[24] The author begins: "That do-in-your-best-friend jealousy could do you a world of good. Here's how your green-eyed monster can deliver the swift kick in the butt you need to go for the gold yourself." Throughout the article, the competitive spirit is lauded with gusto. Of the moral implications of wanting to "do in" a best friend, we hear nothing at all. But then, the overall aim of the article has nothing to do with community and everything to do with ego. We can transform envy from "malicious" into "delicious"; we can make it "work" for us to make sure *we* get what *we* want. If this is the advice being given the readers of popular publications, is it any wonder Wanda Holloway felt so few qualms about wanting to "do in" the person who got in the way of her daughter's (or her own) cheerleading ambitions?

Popular culture does offer a few further tips for handling our envy, apart from the counsel to make it work for us as motivation (which, as far as it goes, is not bad counsel; it simply does not go far enough). These other tips, however, are even more troubling.[25] Some authors suggest we should simply convince ourselves that what our rivals have is not all that desirable. But this kind of discounting sounds more like sour grapes than a true conquest of envy; besides which, how can we genuinely rejoice with our neighbors if we are busy belittling their good fortune in our own minds? Others propose that we minimize our own wants so that we are less likely to be disappointed—and while it is true that striving for simplicity can help to loosen our grip on the stuff that sucks us into status comparisons, we should be careful to distinguish between humble contentment and apathetic resignation.

Despite the limitations of these "tips," the writers of the therapeutic outlook do give us one particularly useful bit of information: namely, a catalog of the *types of wants* that preoccupy our culture sufficiently to become a focus for envy. A survey of titles from popular writings found in late-twentieth-century print media reveals the following: *youth and physical attractiveness* ("Age Cannot Wither Them: Why Envy Is the Reason the Elderly Are Seeking Youth"); *career success* ("I Want What She's Got"); and, of course, *material possessions* ("Gadget Envy").[26] The explosion of digital communications in the twenty-first century has merely made matters worse. Analysts of social media like Facebook have determined that seeing friends enjoying experiences we are not—going to exciting parties or on lavish vacations—results in dissatisfaction with our lives and envy of theirs. Meanwhile, a newly identified "Instagram Envy" appears even more severe, fueled by a steady barrage of idealized images and status updates that together create what researchers are calling FOMO (fear of missing out).[27] This is not, alas, a particularly *impressive* catalog of priorities. If anything, it makes us seem like a brood of overgrown adolescents, frantic in our pursuit of short-lived goods that cannot ultimately give us the satisfaction we desire. Precisely because these goods prove such an empty calorie, we keep hankering after more and more of them, unhappily convinced that our rivals must be getting a bigger and better share. What eating disorders specialist Geneen Roth has said about binge foods seems equally apt to the disordered appetites of envy: "You can never get enough of what you don't really want."[28]

Concluding Questions

But what we want—or what we think we want—is the product of a variety of factors. As we have seen throughout this chapter, our desires are partially *fabricated* ones. For the past hundred years, the machinery of advertising has been running in high gear, purring away in its efforts to convince us that we would be happier if we owned Brand X or more beautiful if we used Brand Y or more socially successful if we drove the automobile or whipped out the smartphone that would make us the envy of our peers—and, not coincidentally, enable us to massage our pride and indulge our greed (since sins tend to travel in packs rather than hunt solo). When the voices of other value-sources have fallen silent, the pitch of the hawkers and hucksters rings out more resoundingly. And when both AdCult and TherapyCult converge in telling us that we *deserve* above all else to feel good about ourselves, what kind of position are we in to argue?

Perhaps if our sense of worth came from looking "up" (to a transcendent source of meaning) or "down" (to the depths of our being) or "back" (to the time-honored wisdom of our traditions) rather than simply *over our shoulders* (at the achievements of our rivals), we would be more immune to such sales pitches. But as it is, our principal way of evaluating our lives lies in comparing ourselves with our neighbors along a fairly trivial checklist of merits (career, appearance, possessions). While we may think we are making these comparisons to ensure we do not end up disadvantaged, the paradoxical truth is quite the contrary: we have been seduced into settling for far too *little*. By diverting our gaze from the moral implications of envy, we have lowered our sights and let our standards shrivel. The combined triumphs of the commercial and the therapeutic have accustomed us to being *less* than we could be, both as individuals and as communities.

What more, then, might we be? Or more specifically, how might our relationships, our character, and our culture be transformed if we exposed the secret sin of envy, recovering for ourselves the insights honed by the time-honored tradition that warned against it as a dangerous vice and, indeed, the second of the seven deadly habits of the heart? Such questions will concern us through the remainder of this book.

Chapter Two

Rival Definitions

Not long ago, I stopped at a traffic light behind a jazzy red sports car whose license plate caught my eye. It read: K'S4U2NV. The driver ("K," I gather) apparently took pleasure in flaunting her possession. But I doubt she really wanted me to suffer because she owned such a vehicle and I did not or to smirk at the prospect that a falling tree limb might flatten her car's shiny chassis. While traditional definitions of envy include both such sadness at others' good fortune and happiness at their ill fortune, perhaps we have progressed so far down the de-moralizing path that we no longer know the meaning of the word.

The point of this chapter is to regain clarity about its meaning. But to do so pulls us in two different directions, one *inclusive* and the other *restrictive*. In closing the previous chapter, I asked how we might benefit from re-moralizing envy, retrieving insights from the tradition that once named it the second of seven deadly sins. This was an inclusive tradition. The framework of the "seven deadlies" collected under a single set of headings a vast array of character traits that distort our relationships with ourselves, one another, the creation, and the divine. Contributors to this tradition technically referred to the seven sins as capital rather than "deadly," because they saw each as a sort of captain, standing at the head (*caput*) of an army of related vices. So, if we are to understand the fullest implications of the traditional label, we must spread our reconnaissance broadly. When we do so, we find that some of the foot soldiers in envy's army bear little surface resemblance to what we initially think of when we hear the word. I will refer to the aspects marshaled under our inclusive definition as Capital Envy or *the invidious spirit*—or simply *invidia*, the Latin name given to the sin.

Once we have identified the diversity and scope of the invidious spirit, however, our attempts at definition become more *restrictive* as we work to distinguish one soldier in the army of Captain Envy from another. Is "envy" really the same thing as "jealousy," for example? Common usage suggests that it is, if we consider a conversation like the following:

Fred: Where are you going for your summer vacation?

Ginger: We're taking a cruise to the Bahamas.

Fred: Wow! I'm jealous.

Yet, the situation implied here is quite different from what we intend when speaking about a "jealous spouse"—or a "jealous God," for that matter. Fearing the loss of a love interest to a rival (jealousy) has different interpersonal and moral dimensions from being upset that a rival already has something we wish we had but do not (envy). Might we not gain greater clarity about our emotional lives if we were more exacting in our terminology?

Moreover, even within the sample categories of jealousy and envy, some experiences seem less morally troubling than others. We can think of instances of benign or even righteous jealousy, or else it would make little sense to speak of Yahweh as a "jealous" God. Rough lines can be drawn between benign and malign forms of envying as well. Does Fred actually hope Ginger's vacation plans will fall through, or does he simply wish he were also going somewhere exciting? Admiration, longing—and even righteous indignation—can all be distinguished from malicious envy. When speaking of the most malicious of envy's versions, I will use the restrictive term "envy proper" (even though such envying is most *improper*, indeed).

Capital Envy

We have already alluded to the fact that philosophical and theological definitions of envy involve a duality of sadness and gladness at the fortune of others, depending on whether that fortune places them one up or one down from us in a status competition. Plato and Aristotle observed this convention among the Greeks; Cicero, among the Romans. In early Christian writings, Basil of Caesarea picked up the theme, and by the time of Thomas Aquinas, it had become standard fare. Thus, in the deadly sins tradition a host of sins related to *malicious glee* march under the banner of Capital Envy: delight in gossip; insincere sympathy; fascination with the faults of others. If Wanda Holloway had succeeded in her plans against Verna and Amber Heath, her rejoicing would have been no less *invidious* (from *invidia*, the Latin word for envy) for the fact that she was finally ahead rather than behind in the cheerleading rivalry.

Religious literature adds further elements to Capital Envy's perverse tendencies to weep with those who rejoice and rejoice with (or rather, *over*) those who weep. The deadly sins tradition depicted each sin not only as a "captain" with his army but also as a "mother" with her daughters or a branch with its withered leaves, all issuing from a common, poisonous root. Pope Gregory the Great specified three other offspring of *invidia*, beyond uncharitable weeping and rejoicing: hatred (think of Wanda Holloway's hostility toward the Heath family), detraction (cutting our neighbors down to size so that we appear larger by comparison), and grumbling (either spreading rumors about someone else's situation or complaining about our own). Later medieval vice diagrams added malice and bitterness to the family tree. (See Figure 2 on p. 22.)

Envy (*invidia*) is the second branch from the bottom on the right. Its pictured "leaves," from left to right, are malice (*malicia*), hatred (*odium*), detraction (*detractio*), grumbling (*sussuratio*), bitterness (*amaritudo*), sadness at the good fortune of others (*afflictio in prosperi*), and rejoicing in ill fortune (*exultatio in adversis*).

It seems clear why a captain with such soldiers, a mother with such children, or a tree with such offshoots would be deemed a serious matter. What is less immediately clear is why, when the earliest lists of deadly or capital vices were devised, envy did not explicitly appear on them. Evagrius Ponticus is given credit for coming up with the first such list in the fourth century CE, for use as a devotional tool by Christian monks living in the Egyptian desert. His version consisted of "eight demonic thoughts," including (in order) gluttony, lust, greed, spiritual sadness, anger, apathy, vainglory, and pride. (See Table 1 on p. 23.) His disciple John Cassian translated the list into Latin for women and men living in religious communities in the Western church and kept an almost identical sequence. Two hundred years later, Gregory modified the list for its first use by Western lay Christians, shifting the order such that pride appeared as the root of all the sins, while greed, gluttony, and lust appeared last. Vainglory, anger, and sadness showed up as numbers one, three, and four. Envy, the newcomer, had shouldered its way up to second place.

Figure 2. Illustrated *Tree of Vices* from a thirteenth-century manuscript of the *Mirror for Virgins* (*Speculum Virginum*) by Conrad of Hirsau, found at the Cistercian abbey of Himmerod in Germany. Source: Walters Art Museum Ms. W.72, fol. 25V. Used under Creative Commons Attribution-ShareAlike 3.0 License: http://creativecommons.org /licenses/by-sa/3.0.

What happened to make envy suddenly appear? Scholars have attempted various answers to the puzzle. One suggested envy was more a matter of concern for Gregory's laypeople than Evagrius's or Cassian's monks and nuns, because of its connection with property.[1] But this does

Table 1. Comparing Capital Sin Lists

EVAGRIUS	CASSIAN	GREGORY
1. *gastrimargia* (gluttony)	1. *gula* (gluttony)	ROOT: *superbia* (pride)
2. *porneia* (lust)	2. *luxuria* (lust)	1. *vana gloria* (vainglory)
3. *filargyria* (greed)	3. *avaritia* (greed)	2. *invidia* (envy)
4. *lupe* (sadness)	4. *ira* (anger)	3. *ira* (anger)
5. *orge* (anger)	5. *tristitia* (sadness)	4. *tristitia* (sadness)
6. *acedia* (apathy)	6. *acedia* (apathy)	5. *avaritia* (greed)
7. *cenodoxia* (vainglory)	7. *inanis gloria* (vainglory)	6. *gula* (gluttony)
8. *hyperephania* (pride)	8. *superbia* (pride)	7. *luxuria* (lust)

not seem right. After all, *greed* is more connected with property than envy, and it appears in the earlier listings. Besides which, many things other than property can provoke envy: a richer prayer life, for example, or a more respected position within a community.

The solution to the puzzle lurks in the ranks of the army of Captain Envy, whose second foot soldier, following classical definitions, is "sadness at the good fortune of others." If we look back at the lists, we see *sadness* (*lupe* or *tristitia*) in fourth place for Evagrius, and fifth, for Cassian. An audience schooled in the classics would have made this connection immediately, recognizing envy as kin to other forms of sorrow brought on by anxiety, annoyance, or insult. The farther removed we are from those classics, however, the more the linkage must be called to our attention. Pope Gregory I decided that his audience needed particular schooling in the type of hostile sadness brought on by status comparisons, namely *envy*. Thus, he set it apart from the more passive sadness (*tristitia*) that eventually collapses into *sloth*.

Gregory's placement of *envy* as capital sin number two is no accident. Biblically speaking, it is the second sin committed in the troubled history of humanity: no sooner are Adam and Eve expelled from the garden for their prideful disobedience than Cain kills Abel out of envy that God preferred his younger brother's sacrifice. But Gregory's placement also recognizes that envy is a sin we must address early in our spiritual journeys. First, of course, we must deal with our tendencies to think more highly of ourselves than we merit, or we will not embark on any program of self-development at all. After this, how many other deadly sins would loosen their grip if we could rest content with the distinctive gifts we have been given, abandoning our unhappy comparisons with others? How much anger grows out of a conviction of injured merit, a fist-shaking "*I* deserve better!"? How much greed springs from an ache of inner insufficiency? How much indulgence in excessive food or exploitative sexuality emerges out of efforts to salve a wounded and insecure ego? How much sloth is the dying whimper: "If the deck is stacked against me, I might as well not try at all"?

The Eyes Have It

It is, then, no coincidence that *invidia* appears as sin number two in Gregory's list of seven deadlies. In fact, this placement seems like a hidden joke: how Capital Envy must hate consistently coming in second, never getting to be number one. Alas for envy, Gregory's sequence remains the standard for subsequent literary treatments of the deadly sins, as we will see in chapter 4—for Dante's climb up Mount Purgatory or the Parson's sermon from Chaucer's *Canterbury Tales*.

Even the word Gregory chose to name the sin is no coincidence. For the Greeks, one of the most frequent words used for envying was *phthonos*, stemming from a root verb (*phthio*) meaning "wither" or "pine away." How apt this is for naming how we feel when we pine for something we cannot have or shrivel at the thought of a rival's flourishing. Think of the frequently quoted line from novelist Gore Vidal: "Whenever a friend succeeds, a little something in me dies."[2] In languages deriving from Latin, the word roots are no less telling. *Invidia* (the basis for Spanish *envidia*, French *envie*, and English *envy*) combines an intensifying prefix, *in*, with *videre*, "to see." This also makes experiential sense. After all, envy is fundamentally concerned with perceived differences in status between the self and a rival, and vision is our readiest means of arriving at such perceptions.

Many cultures reflect this connection between envy and seeing through the concept of the *evil eye*. In such cultures, prosperity must be protected from the potentially damaging gaze of the other. Brides wear veils to conceal their beauty and happiness. Children are smeared with dirt or given unflattering nicknames as if to show how little their parents care. Compliments are deflected. The evil eye notion even appears in the Bible: it is *ra ayin* in Hebrew (Deut. 28:54) and *ophthalmos poneros* in Greek (Mark 7:22).[3] Indeed, lest we think that evil eye imagery simply characterizes "primitive" cultures, it is worth considering how it lingers in our own psyches. Why else would common speech patterns include an idiom like "to look daggers at" another person or the wishfully lethal "if looks could kill"? What on earth could we mean by a bizarre toast like "Here's mud in your eye!" unless perhaps we intend it as token protection against the evil eye of envy?[4]

The "eyes have it" in still another common idiom for envy: the "green-eyed monster." To be accurate, this expression originally referred to *jealousy* rather than envy in the context of Iago's words to Othello in Shakespeare's play. But because of general slippage between the concepts of envy and jealousy and because of the kindred expression "to be green with envy," the idiom has stuck. It bears noting, however, that the green of envy is not the spring-like color of hope and new life. Rather, it is the sickly color of bilious or jaundiced skin tone. In fact, the German language idiom speaks of an envious person as turning yellow (the literal color of jaundice) rather than green: *Er wurde gelb vor Neid.*

Nether, Nether Land

The German word for envy in this idiom opens another window onto aspects of the experience. *Neid* comes from the same roots as our word "nether," or "lower." The "netherworld," located beneath the earth's surface, is another term for the infernal regions, the underworld of the dead. To feel envy is to suffer the torments of hell, even if it is a hell of our own making.

In addition to "lower," the Old English root for "nether" also means "abyss." This, too, rings true to experience. The pangs of envy are *abysmal*; they ream us out, leaving us feeling hollow inside. As a fifth century BCE Cynic philosopher wrote, "As oxide eats up iron, so are the envious devoured by this passion."[5] Even today, seeing us in torment, a friend might ask, "What's eating you?"

By the Christian Renaissance, the connection between envy and self-devouring had achieved iconic status. The German artist Hans Weiditz crafted a woodcut entitled "Envy," which depicted a figure clutching its heart in her hands, devouring it as if it were an oversized apple.[6] "Vice trees" drawn to illustrate the seven deadly sins showed *pride* with her mirror, *avarice* with her money chest, *gluttony* with his beer stein, *anger* with his sword . . . and *envy* with his heart in his hand, raising it to his lips for a bittersweet bite. (See Figure 3.) Further exploration of such "arresting images" will occupy us in chapter 3.

Envy Proper

So far in this chapter, we have explored an inclusive array of impulses that march under the banner of Capital Envy, a banner whose coat of arms includes a jaundiced eye, an underworld abyss, and a person devouring her own heart. Now we turn to questions leading to more restrictive definitions. What is envy proper, for example, as distinct from innocent manifestations of healthy competition? How is it distinct from kindred hurtful experiences like coveting, jealousy, or resentment? The clearer our definitions, the better we will be at diagnosing harmful envy in ourselves and our communities, and the more effective at working toward prevention and healing.

Figure 3. Anonymous illustration for Boccacio, *Concerning Famous Women* (*De claris mulieribus*), 1487, Louvain edition. Source: Eric de Bruyn (2001), *De vergeten beeldtaal van Jheronimus Bosch*. Used under Creative Commons Attribution/Share-Alike License: http://commons.wikimedia.org/wiki/File:De_claris_mulieribus_001.jpg.

Here is a basic definition, for further unpacking: Envy proper is the pained perception of an unfavorable difference in status between the self and a rival on a scale of personally significant values, accompanied by a desire to correct the imbalance by raising the self or lowering the other (or both).

First, envy proper is a "pained perception." Its feeling tone is primarily sadness, though sometimes tinged with anger and hostility. It relies on differences perceived to be the case, though these perceptions may only be in the eye of the beholder and may well be distorted.

Second, envy focuses on status comparisons with personally significant rivals. When we are envious, we think we can be good only by being better than someone else. The "someone else" chosen for our comparison purposes tends to follow norms of proximity, to be someone more or less "in our league."[7] Thus, Wanda Holloway obsesses over Amber Heath, not the Dallas Cowboy cheerleaders; I am more likely to fixate on the publication record of a colleague at another small liberal arts college than one at a major research university. Further, we envy only regarding matters significant to our scale of values: Wanda Holloway would no more envy an extensive list of publications than I would envy selection to a cheerleading squad.

Third, envy is so pained by the status differences it perceives that enviers feel driven to change their situation. If we experience ourselves as powerful enough to improve our lot, moments of envy will be of fairly short duration. In such situations, in fact, an initial moment of pining (remember the Greek *phthonos*) can help us identify what matters in our lives, motivating us to pursue such goals more vigorously. But if we feel powerless, our remaining option is to downgrade the other to help ourselves feel better. Hence, the belittling and grumbling activities identified by Gregory the Great among *invidia*'s "daughters." Hence, acts of vandalism that destroy possessions, even when we stand to gain no comparable possessions for ourselves. Hence, character assassination—or the attempted actual assassination of the Texas Cheerleader Murder plot.

Benign vs. Malign Envy

The preceding definition helps us differentiate envy proper from more benign attitudes and actions. "Upgrading" the self is significantly different from "downgrading" a rival; a wish to emulate differs from a wish to harm. Indeed, "emulation" is the term used in English to convey Aristotle's classical category for healthier forms of competition.[8] The contrast in Greek is between *phthonos*, the "withering" desire to thwart our rivals, and *zelos*, the ardent desire to be like them. Some fifteen hundred years later, in the Christian tradition, Aquinas picked up on Aristotle by differentiating *zelus* or "zeal" as energy directed toward pursuing a desirable quality from *zelus invidiae*, or the "zeal of envy."[9] The arena of athletics is one in which we see such distinctions clearly. Some time-honored rivalries work to spur each player to greater heights of performance: Magic Johnson and Larry Bird in professional basketball; Peyton Manning and Tom Brady in football; Chris Evert and Martina Navratilova in tennis. Contrast these relationships with the Tonya Harding/Nancy Kerrigan debacle from the 1994 U.S. Figure Skating Championships: the invidiously "zealous" attempt by Harding's former husband and bodyguard to keep Kerrigan from skating by hiring someone to break her leg.

An additional factor in making the benign/malign distinction relates to the first part of our definition of "envy proper," its "pained perspective." "Admiration" is not pained by seeing another's better fortune; "emulation" is not hostile when a rival is temporarily further along a path to achievement. In his *Theory of Justice*, political philosopher John Rawls defines both "emulative envy," which actively attempts to achieve what others have without begrudging their having it, and a more passive "benign envy," which simply affirms the value of something another person has and we do not.[10] If we think back to Fred and Ginger's imagined interaction about her upcoming cruise to the Bahamas, Rawls's latter term comes closest to identifying Fred's reaction (though it would sound odd for him to respond, "Wow! I'm benignly envious," rather than the less precise, "Wow! I'm jealous").

Two other "pained" but benign emotions are related to envy but distinct from "envy proper." One of these is *longing*. When we pine for something (recall the Greek *phthonos* again), we may feel sad at not possessing it. Still, we do not experience someone else's possession as personally demeaning. We can, therefore, long for a loving relationship or a meaningful job—or, less loftily, an exotic vacation—without envying another person who has one. "Longing" does not fit the middle prong of the envy proper definition: it does not concern itself with status comparisons. The other "pained" but distinguishable affect is *indignation*, . . . but this topic requires its own subheading.

Indignation vs. Envy Proper

Aristotle, again, helps with a clear distinction. He points out that indignation resembles envy insofar as both involve "a disturbing pain excited by the prosperity of others."[11] But indignation is aroused when our sense of justice is violated, either because the other's success is unmerited or because our lack of success results from unfairness. Thus, while a coworker might label us "envious" of goods she purchased with embezzled funds, we would insist that we are not envious but righteously indignant. While some might accuse the poor of envying the rich, if the poverty results from a deck stacked unfairly against certain members of society, the matter in question is not so much envy as indignation. This distinction will become particularly important in chapter 6 when we examine charges that people who call for higher taxes on the upper 1 percent of the population are motivated by a "politics of envy." For the moment, though, we will focus on three other things: the classical concept of indignation, its distinctive "grammar," and its tendency, despite our best efforts at clear distinctions, to slip down the continuum from benign to malign.

First, the concept. Aristotle's distinctive term for indignation is the Greek word *nemesis*. In modern-day English, we use the same word to mean something like "deserved comeuppance" as, for example: "In the wily Inspector Hercule Poirot, the crook finally met his nemesis." At its root, though, *nemesis* derives from a verb meaning "distribute," and one's nemesis is one's fair share. The Greek poet Hesiod personified Nemesis as a goddess of distributive justice, responsible for seeing that individuals received their due. It is not a far stretch to see why Aristotle chose this name for the emotion we feel when justice has been violated, in someone else's favor or our disfavor.

The grammar of indignation is distinct from that of envy. It makes no grammatical sense to say that we are envious "on behalf of" someone else. Even Wanda Holloway was not envious on behalf of her daughter; the stake in the cheerleading competition was clearly the mother's own sense of self-worth. On the other hand, we can be indignant on behalf of a third party, since the issue at stake is fairness and not competitive self-image. And while the object of envy is always a person or group of people, indignation can just as readily be about a state of affairs. We may, for example, be indignant at or about a supervisor's falsely accusing subordinates of wrongdoing to cover his own incompetence. What is at stake in indignation is a principle of fairness, not a one-up or one-down relationship.

Even though such distinctions matter, we must still be cautious. The continuum from benign to malign versions of envy is slippery and paved with self-deception. Fairness is not always clear; one person's more equitable tax code is another's scheme to "soak the rich." Further, indignation can all too easily become a mask for less righteous feelings. We claim we want justice when really we just want some benefit for ourselves: or, worst-case scenario, we may simply want the more fortunate to suffer deprivation out of spite.

Spite, Schadenfreude, and Resentment vs. Envy Proper

Spite is, indeed, another foot soldier in the army of Capital Envy, but along with its unsavory companions Schadenfreude and resentment, it can still be distinguished from envy proper. Coming from the same root as "despise," spite looks on others with malice. Far from loving their neighbors, spiteful people feel an urge to hurt or humiliate them or in some other way to "get even." Aristotle differentiated spite from indignation by pointing out that nemesis is pained by the undeserved misfortune of others, while malice feels pleasure at such misfortune.[12] Spite rejoices in the wrong. The word in Greek tells us so: *epichairekakia* combines *chairo*, "rejoicing," with *kako*, "bad or evil."

English does not have a word that so conveniently combines these two roots, but German does. Schadenfreude puts together *Schaden*, "hurt, harm, wrong" and *Freude*, "joy, pleasure." Schadenfreude names the smug satisfaction we may feel when a moralistic televangelist is caught in a compromising situation in a motel room. Schadenfreude would have described Wanda Holloway's glee had something disqualified Amber Heath instead of her own daughter from the Channelview cheerleading competition.

Both spite and Schadenfreude emerge out of a skewed sense of justice: spite wants to even the score; Schadenfreude delights when someone is brought down a peg. A third member of this family, resentment, also claims justice as its aim. Like indignation, resentment is angry over treatment perceived as unfair. But where indignation focuses outward, seeking to right wrongs, resentment focuses inward. Resentment thrives on "re-feeling" any injury it has experienced.[13] It chews the cud of unhappiness over and over, squeezing out the bitter juices, swallowing the pulp only to vomit it back up and chew some more. Indignation draws itself up to its full height while resentment hunches in on itself. The eye of indignation blazes, that of resentment narrows and glares.

Over time, the issue for resentment ceases to be the wrong that provoked it and becomes instead the fact of its own suffering. Thus, the object of resentment is not, as with envy proper, a good belonging to another; rather, it is a wound belonging to the self. In envy, I feel deprived; in resentment, I feel wronged. Unlike envy, as well, resentment often focuses less on a specific rival than on a generalized group, an unidentified "they" involved in rigging "the system" and thwarting my chances for success. Finally, like spite, resentment bears a strong vindictive streak, a fist-shaking "I'll get them for this!" If resentful people come into positions of power, the retaliatory results can be disastrous.

Jealousy vs. Envy Proper

More than resentment, spite, or Schadenfreude, the emotion generating the greatest confusion on the family tree of envy is jealousy. I noted this a few pages ago in Fred and Ginger's imagined interchange about her upcoming cruise; yet, I also admitted it would sound odd for Fred to respond to Ginger, "Wow! I'm benignly envious" instead of the more common, "Wow! I'm jealous." On many occasions in our lives, verbal exactness does not matter very much. But on some occasions, it does. If I phone my administrative assistant to let her know I will be absent from work, it is enough to say I have the flu. But if I talk to my doctor, I need to be more specific about my symptoms.

This book is intended more in the nature of a doctor's office conversation than an administrative update. We are not simply concerned to make broad excuses for our conduct; we want a more precise diagnosis of our condition. As we saw in chapter 1, over the past hundred years cultural forces have seduced us into overlooking the sinful dimensions of envying and provoking envy. How can we resist such seduction if we do not know exactly what envy is? Moreover, if exposing this secret sin to the light persuades us that envy does pose a moral problem, surely the more we know about what it is and is not, the better our chances will be for finding a cure.

So: what is the difference between jealousy and envy proper? A standard distinction goes this way: "Jealousy fears to lose what it has; envy is pained at seeing another have what it wants for itself."[14] This contrast widens our perspective to include uses of the term "jealous" that we overlook in a preoccupation with *romantic* jealousy. For example, we might say that an author is "jealous" in guarding her writing time against all interruptions. (Contrast this with an author who is "envious" of someone whose lighter workload produces fewer interruptions to start with.) This broader use of jealous also helps us see its verbal connection to the Latin *zelus* or Greek *zelos*. We can be said to be either "jealous of" or "zealous for" some worthy attribute, such as our reputation.

The idea of zealous protectiveness also explains why Hebrew Scripture speaks of Yahweh as a "jealous" God. The loyalty of all creatures rightfully belongs to the Lord, who justifiably seeks to protect the covenant relationship. We might say something similar about a "jealous" spouse: insofar as a marriage involves commitments to fidelity, then partners rightfully resist having that commitment threatened.

There are, then, more or less legitimate forms of jealousy. There are also more or less rational experiences of it. In extremes of irrational jealousy, a person may fear to lose a relationship that exists only in the imagination. Thus, a stalker may be horrified when a love object appears in public with a new partner. While in actuality, the stalker does not have a relationship that is in jeopardy, in fantasy he does. Thus, he is not simply *envious* at seeing another person have what he wants for himself; he is also *jealous* at feeling threatened by a rival. Other analysts of jealousy therefore speak of it as involving a "wariness of being supplanted"—most characteristically experienced in personal relationships.[15] Perhaps, indeed, this is the reason that we generally find it easier to say "I'm jealous" than "I'm envious," even in contexts where the latter would be more precise. To speak of jealousy is to identify oneself as a "lover," a possessor of something prized and worth protecting. To speak of envy, in contrast, is to identify as a "loser," a peg below a rival on some status ladder and petty enough to care. Othello, the jealous character in Shakespeare's play, is tragic yet somehow noble; Iago, the envious one, is simply vile.

Coveting vs. Envy Proper

The last of the invidious dispositions to attract our attention in this chapter of rival definitions is *covetousness*. Like jealousy, it bears a strong-enough resemblance to envy that the two are sometimes mistaken for one another. In terms of word roots, though, "coveting" links to the Latin *cupere*, "to desire." A synonym for avarice or greed, "cupidity" has its own place on lists of the seven deadly sins, though admittedly, it often travels in close company with envy. Coveting also appears among the Ten Commandments. Its object is most commonly a material thing (the Bible's prohibition against coveting the neighbor's wife hails from a culture in which a wife was more property than person).

"Envy proper" has a broader range of objects. I can envy my neighbor's popularity, paycheck, promotion—or her daughter's cheerleading prowess. Depending on my values, any of these can make me feel bested in a competition. However, the more an envy-appeal in advertising stimulates us to crave consumer goods as a means of marking our success, and the more our culture teaches us to define who we *are* by what we *own*, the more the lines between covetousness and envy tend to blur.

Strictly speaking, though, coveting wants another person's possessions whereas envy wants the status they confer—or simply wants the other not to have the status advantage. Coveting a neighbor's new car can be satisfied by getting one just like it: the issue is *what* the neighbor has, not *that* the neighbor has it. Envying, perversely, can be just as satisfied if the rival's car is stolen or seriously damaged.

Making this point in a pithy way, sociologist Helmut Schoeck observes, "The thief is covetous; the arsonist is envious."[16] He offers this news story as an example. A man arrested for setting fire to eight automobiles told the police, "I couldn't afford to own [a car], and I didn't want anyone else to have one." But setting fires is not the only type of destructive act that emerges out of envy: any act of vandalism will do; indeed, I suspect the creation of computer malware roots in a similar dynamic. According to Schoeck, criminal law in English-speaking countries defines vandalism as "senseless and malicious" damage to property, "without any material gain to the perpetrator." One way of making sense of such senselessness, however, is to ponder the possibility of an envy motive, a desire to lash out at those whose superior advantages are experienced as putting the self to shame.

Coveting and envy proper can thus be distinguished as the impulse to *acquire* versus the impulse to *spoil*. But the two experiences do overlap. Consider a story that figured in North Carolina newspapers in the late 1990s. One headline read: "Home Envy Killer Gets Life after Jury Deadlocks."[17] The "home envy killer" in question, Shelby Jean White, shot and beat to death a sixty-year-old widow whose house she had wanted to buy but could not afford. Given the distinctions we have just been drawing, the newspaper headline might more accurately have spoken of a "Home-*Coveting* Killer"; the narrative of events shows that White was obsessed with acquiring the specific piece of property, no matter the means required. A contrast between Wanda Holloway and Shelby Jean White comes to mind: where the Texan wanted to punish her rival for making Holloway feel inferior, the North Carolinian wanted to eliminate her rival in order to take possession of the other woman's belongings. It is, though, reasonable to speculate that White's motives also bore something of the pain of seeing a neighbor enjoy a success she felt she could not attain. While distinct in theory, in practice envy and coveting mutually reinforce each other.

We see this mutual reinforcement most tragically among our youth. In a culture that measures our merit by the size of our paycheck and the shape of our bodies, doing little to promote spiritual virtues like compassion and generosity and much to promote consumerist values (like "whoever dies with the most toys wins"), young people are especially vulnerable. Advertising stirs up covetous longings for bigger and better, newer and shinier goods; this covetousness blends into envy of the objects' proud possessors. Popular writer Nancy Friday vividly describes this tragedy of our de-moralized society: "Envy," she writes, "has become so familiar that children pick up guns and kill other children to steal the gold chain or the running shoes, or just to dissipate the rankling inferiority that envy produces."[18] Yet, we can scarcely stand in judgment unless we are also ready to expose our secret sin to the light, teaching and practicing a different set of values in our own individual and communal lives.

What's Next?

Through the course of this chapter, we have reviewed the troops marshaled under the banner of Capital Envy, carefully distinguishing one from another out of a conviction that precise diagnosis of an affliction is important for effective cure. With the exceptions of appreciative emulation, righteous indignation, and some forms of legitimate jealousy, envy's affiliates show kindred destructive dynamics. They fixate on comparisons, obsessively calculating their own advantage or disadvantage, viewing the other chiefly as rival rather than as neighbor. They interpret the world of goods as a fixed pie, such that *more* for someone else invariably means *less* for me, yet paradoxically approach creation as an inexhaustible resource to exploit in the competition for status. These hurtful emotions squint up our eyes, eat out our hearts, and turn us a sickly green.

When Gregory I put evil-eyed envy in second place on his list of seven deadly sins, he marked it as a matter of great moral seriousness for Christians of former generations. Artists who painted frescoes on church walls or produced engravings for private devotions portrayed it in highly unflattering terms—quite the opposite of the seductive portrait used in the envy-appeal of recent advertising. A look back at these earlier arresting images will remind us of what we have lost in our understanding of vices and virtues—and what we might meaningfully regain.

Chapter Three

Arresting Images

Despite all the ways in which twenty-first century youth are different from the lay "consumers" of the medieval cardinal sins tradition, the two groups share one strong similarity: both participate in cultures that are largely *pictorial.* My students, for example, may not always be adept at analyzing written texts. However, having cut their perceptual eyeteeth on television, computers, and video games, they are amazingly keen at reading images. If I project any kind of pictorial representation in class, even my sleepiest sophomores will notice details that I, the print-bound professor, will have missed. While written prose often bores them, they unfailingly "get" the picture.

Likewise goes for our ancestors in the pre-print culture of the Middle Ages. For the centuries stretching from Gregory the Great to Gutenberg, lay-people received major portions of their religious and moral instruction from sculpture and stained glass, frescoes and illuminations. Through such visual media, they absorbed biblical narratives and key events in salvation history; they viewed examples of behaviors to practice and behaviors to shun; they witnessed the promised rewards for a life of virtue and punishments for a life of vice. Envy, as one of seven deadly sins and as a vice opposed to the theological virtue of charity or love, was a frequent focus for concern. Visual images assigned to it were so vivid that they continue to crop up in our colloquial vocabularies, even if we have long since forgotten their origins.

Christian Education Curriculum

In 1215, the Fourth Lateran Council decreed that all Christians should make thorough confession to a priest at least once a year. Shortly thereafter, itinerant bands of newly licensed Franciscan and Dominican preachers and confessors began making their way across the continent of Europe and through the British Isles. In the English-speaking world, moreover, the Lambeth Constitutions of 1281 required all parish priests to provide instruction four times a year on key elements of the Christian faith, including the Apostles' Creed, the Ten Commandments, the Lord's Prayer, and the seven deadly sins. As a result, a demand arose for a new genre of publications: preachers' manuals, complete with teaching tips for administering the newly mandated Christian education curriculum.

In a culture where literacy was rare, pictures were worth thousands of words. Thus, preacher's handbooks were filled with illustrations—not only verbal ones in the form of "telling tales" (which we will visit in chapter 4) but also hand-drawn illuminations to assist in bringing moral and theological lessons to life. In the fourteenth century, such manuals spread from a clerical to a lay audience in the form of Poor Man's Bibles, psalters, books of hours, and other private moral and devotional works.

To the medieval mind, such illustrated books carried more than educational value: some people even thought they carried magical properties. In the private devotional life of the medieval Christian, according to historian Georges Duby, "sacred belongings of small size"—whether illustrated Bible stories or pictures of vices and virtues—supplied a "portable setting," a kind of laptop altar, for engaging in meditative practices thought to give protection against evil powers.[1] For the vaster audience that could not afford to purchase hand-illuminated miniatures, woodcuts—printed paper illustrations that could be carried in a pocket or pinned to a wall—provided a less expensive alternative. Thus, if a medieval couple displayed in their home the caricature of a hideously squint-eyed and venom-spewing Dame Envy, not only were they reminding themselves to keep their prying eyes and gossiping tongues in check but they might also even be setting up a shield to keep envious spirits away.

Nor should we underestimate the pure entertainment value of such caricatures. In their details, many images of the vices reflected a medieval fondness for burlesque. Such satirical contents even made their way into church art and architecture, appearing in carvings on choir stalls and baptismal fonts; in sculpted capitals on columns and tympana over doorways; on stained glass windows; on tapestries and wall paintings. These visual aids served up moral lessons arresting enough to captivate the most diverse of audiences.

Sin Wheels

A frequent visual aid for instruction in the seven deadly sins took the form of the "sin wheels," ranging from elaborate diagrams constructed for religious professionals to cruder images intended to grab the attention of the laity. Hugh of St. Victor's schema of the "five sevens" gave rise to diagrams of the former type.[2] In addition to the deadly sins, the "five sevens" include the gift virtues of Isaiah 11, the petitions of the Lord's Prayer, and the Beatitudes divided into two "sevens": the blessed ones ("those who mourn," for example), and the blessing they will receive ("for they shall be comforted"). The deadly sins are further surrounded by the names of their (seven or more) offspring. Envy's children are those we would expect from the previous chapter: joy at a neighbor's ill fortune, sorrow at a neighbor's good fortune, malice, bitterness, detraction, grumbling, and hate.

The tiny picture of envy in one diagram of Hugh's "five sevens" follows the classical precedent of depicting aspects of the soul as female—not to suggest that women are more prone to sin than men but to reflect the fact that both the Latin *anima* and Greek *psyche* are grammatically feminine. Envy is holding her right hand over her eyes and pointing with the other at something to the viewer's left. Covering the eyes is highly symbolic, as we recall from chapter 2. Envy involves intense visual scrutiny, constantly measuring the neighbor's goods against our own, until we are so pained by the contrast, we can no longer bear to look. Equally symbolic is the pointing finger: if we follow it across the diagram we see a seated Dame Greed, smugly clutching bags of treasure. Thus, not only is Dame Envy showing us precisely what she is sad not to possess. More than that, she is wordlessly "grumbling" or gossiping, lessening her own distress by pointing out the foibles of her neighbor.

The satiric attitude of the scholarly illumination of the "five sevens" carries over to a less scholarly image for the laity, found in a church painting at Ingatestone in Great Britain.[3] What is known of this painting today comes from a drawing made of it by a transcriber before a later age took offense at the satire and—alas for our sakes—saw fit to cover it with whitewash. According to the transcription, envy appears in second place, just after pride in a counterclockwise rotation. The unnamed painter has shifted from allegorical images to real-life vignettes and so is no longer restricted to female personifications for the soul. Instead, envy is depicted by four men, dressed in a fashion displaying a certain amount of wealth, standing before two gloved and bewigged judges. No money appears to be changing hands, so the scene is probably not of bribery. It is more likely a case of false witness—of malice and bitterness sufficient to haul a rival to court in a vengeful attempt to get even. This medieval illustration might well prompt us to wonder how much litigation in our own society is spawned by invidious motives.

Vice Trees

The sin wheels that raise such provocative questions derive some of their meaning from the metaphor of life as a circle that goes round and round, spiraling upward toward God or downward toward the devil and engaging us in intersecting patterns of virtues or vices along the way. Other metaphors also arose to describe the course of human living—the metaphor of fruit-bearing, for example. A good life bears good fruit. But bad seeds and wicked roots give rise to poisonous "vice trees."

Diagrammatic trees of vices and virtues became popular in the twelfth century. Over the next hundred years, according to Jennifer O'Reilly, they came to be reproduced on classroom walls in the universities of Paris and Oxford, like the pull-down maps of the Holy Land still found in low-tech seminary classrooms.[4] We have already seen two examples of such trees as illustrations in chapter 2: one from a thirteenth-century instructional manual for nuns, showing all the sub-sins dangling off their respective sin branches like so many dead leaves, and one from a book "On Famous Women," with small figurines for each vice embedded in the tree's foliage.

Tree diagrams offered the convenience of a comprehensive ethical system whose implications were clear: merely pulling off a few dead leaves or rotten fruits—repenting of a few misdeeds, amending a few bad habits—would not suffice to create a life of virtue. The axe must be laid to the root of the whole poisoned organism (Luke 3:9). An illumination from an encyclopedia written about 1120 makes this point graphically.[5] On one page, a flowering tree of goodness grows from sinuous roots woven elegantly around a portrait of Lady Charity, understood to be the source of all virtues. On the facing page, a barren tree of evil grows from a root that seems to be hollowed out by a circle bearing the word "Greed"—and on either side of the "bad tree," an axe bites into the ground.

Other vice trees follow Gregory's pattern of putting not Greed but Pride at the root of all other sins. The remaining seven—vainglory, envy, anger, sadness, gluttony, and lust—sprout from seven branches off a central trunk, three per side and one at the top. Many of these diagrams exist in facing-page pairings, opposite trees whose branches name the four cardinal and three theological virtues (prudence, justice, temperance, fortitude, and faith, hope, love). While structurally similar, vice and virtue trees differ in a few significant respects. Often, Christ (the New Adam) emerges from the virtue tree's crown, whereas the summit of the vice tree is occupied by the Old Adam, crossing his arms across his bare chest to conceal the nakedness of which he has grown ashamed. Vice trees are encircled by serpents or flanked by dragons; virtue trees, by angels. Vice branches and their deadly leaves droop, but the branches of virtue arch upward, as if straining toward heaven. Likewise, the leaf medallions naming subsidiary virtues bob, like helium balloons, toward the sky.

A particularly imaginative vice tree appears in a miniature drawn to illustrate the thirteenth-century devotional book *Mirror of Life and Death* (*Miroir de vie et de mort*). This picture shows a tree with sevenfold *roots* rather than sevenfold branches.[6] Each root ends in the shape of a serpent with a woman's head. The names of the seven deadly sins are written beside these busts, but the labels are scarcely necessary. Each vice bears her own familiar attribute: pride with her mirror, gluttony with her stein, avarice with her money-box, and so on. Envy, pointedly, bears a gnawing animal in her bosom, eating her heart out once again.

Giotto and the Scrovegni Chapel

In many of the vice trees and sin wheels just described, the depiction evolves from diagrams heavy with words (like Hugh of St. Victor's five sevens) to pictorial genre scenes—a move paralleling the emergence of the deadly sins tradition from the monastery into the mainstream of popular piety. Designs for such genre scenes came from multiple sources: narrative epic poems, miracle and mystery plays, visions of the saints, various collections of legends and Bible stories. Some scholars have speculated that traveling medieval craftspeople transposed images from one medium to another: from wall painting to stained glass window to doorway carving—a theory that helps account for significant, cross-regional similarities in depicting common themes.[7] A churchgoer in northern England could thus find herself visually quite at home in a sanctuary in central Germany or southern France.

Most of the medieval artists responsible for such templates remain unidentified, until we arrive at one of the most original and arresting images of envy ever drawn. The work is by the pre-Renaissance Florentine master, Giotto di Bondone (1267?-1337). The image appears in one of his earliest and best-known works: the fresco cycle in the Scrovegni or Arena Chapel in Padua, Italy. Unlike any illustration we have examined up to this point, Giotto's "portrait" of Envy—even with its clearly allegorical elements—appears as a rounded, dimensional human figure rather than a flat, stylized form.

Enrico Scrovegni commissioned the construction of a chapel next to his family palace. Dedicated to the Virgin of Charity, the chapel was intended in part to expiate the usury of his father, Reginaldo, who was so infamous that Dante, a contemporary and compatriot, consigned him to the seventh circle of the *Inferno*.[8] To accomplish such expiation, sins of greed receive focal attention in the chapel's artistic program. But envy also takes a prominent place.

The chapel is entered through doors in the west wall, on which a vivid fresco of the Last Judgment appears. Themes of condemnation and blessing continue on the north and south walls: the north, at the left hand of Christ in the Last Judgment, contains portraits of vices; the south, in exacting counterpoint, presents portraits of virtues. The cardinal virtues of patience, fortitude, temperance, and justice face off against their contraries, foolishness, inconstancy, wrath, and injustice; the theological virtues of faith, charity, and hope square off against faithlessness, envy, and despair.

Envy appears second closest to the scene of the Last Judgment. Directly above it is a portrayal of Christ's ascent to Calvary and the crucifixion—to which, according to the Gospels, he was given up by the chief priests and the crowd "out of envy" (Matt. 27:18 and Mark 15:10). Yet higher in the same niche is a fresco of the young Jesus disputing with the rabbis in the Temple—a moment which may have first stirred their envy of his learning.

Giotto's personification of Envy is quite an "arresting" figure. Like all the vices, she is painted in monotonous, chalky gray, creating the illusion of carved stone. The only touch of color evident in her portrait is the red of flames surrounding her feet—a hint of the coming flames of hell. In her left hand, the allegorized figure clutches a moneybag. With a talon-like right hand, she gropes after more, always more. (See Figure 4.)

In these attributes, Dame Envy contrasts dramatically with Lady Charity, directly opposite her across the nave of the chapel. (See Figure 5.) Moneybags lie at the latter's feet, where either she has cast them in utter disregard or they await her distribution in alms to the poor. In her right hand, she holds a bowl of fruit—either the metaphoric fruits of her virtue

Figure 4. Giotto, *Envy* (*Invidia*), Scrovegni Chapel, Padua. Used under Creative Commons Attribution /Share-Alike License, http://commons .wikimedia.org/wiki/File:Giotto _-_Scrovegni_-_-48-_-_Envy.jpg.

Figure 5. Giotto, *Charity* (*Karitas*), Scrovegni Chapel, Padua. Used under Creative Commons Attribution/Share -Alike License: http://commons .wikimedia.org/wiki/File:Giotto _-_Scrovegni_-_-45-_-_Charity.jpg.

or actual food that she is prepared to give away. Most telling of all, where the outstretched hand of Envy ends in grasping claws, the up-reaching left hand of Charity holds a heart that she offers to God (who, in miniature, reaches down from the top-right corner of the fresco to receive it). Thus, in contrast to Envy who, as we have seen in other renderings, *eats her heart out* in self-consuming torment, here in Giotto's fresco, Charity gives her heart away in self-sacrificing joy.

But it is the face of Giotto's Envy that contains the most visually unforgettable details. Her head, shown in profile, reveals an elongated ear, a bit like a donkey's, protruding backward and meeting with a horn that pokes out from her turban and curls toward her neck. The implication is that envy demonizes and bestializes us, making us less than human in our eagerness to hear bad news about the rivals whom we wish ill. But even more destructively, envy turns us into vipers, avid in our belittling and backbiting, grumbling and gossiping, attempting to poison our neighbors' reputations so that we may look better by comparison. Thus, a snake emerges from Envy's mouth, with its own jaws open, ready to strike. Yet, in a supreme irony, the serpent has coiled around to bite Envy herself in the eye. In short, the vice of *invidia* hurts no one so much as the person who is envying, and once again the scrutinizing eyes of *in* + *videre* become the focus for its most excruciating pain.[9]

Dogs, Bones, and Hieronymus Bosch

After Giotto, many Renaissance masters continued to be fascinated with the theme of vices and virtues, laden with symbolic riches and profound implications for the fate of the human soul. While Giotto created his vice list from contraries to the cardinal and theological virtues, other artists favored the list of seven capital vices created by Gregory the Great. One of the best-known visual portrayals of the seven deadlies of all time appears in a work by the late-fifteenth-century Netherlandish artist Hieronymus Bosch (1450?–1516). Because it is rendered on an actual table top, the painting is sometimes referred to as *The Table of Wisdom*.

At first glance, Bosch's painting calls to mind something we have seen before: the "sin wheels" of medieval fame. Like them, he arranges the vices in a circle whose center encloses an image of God: not God the Father enthroned, as in some illustrations of Hugh of St. Victor's "five sevens," but Christ arising from the tomb, showing the viewer the wounds in his hands and side. Vignettes (called *tondi*) in each of the four corners of Bosch's composition show the "last things" awaiting the individual soul: death, final judgment, and entrance into heaven or punishment in hell.

In attending to this theme of final judgment, a striking innovation compels our attention. From a distance, Bosch's sin wheel actually looks like an eyeball: the central circle forms the pupil; the ring of radii around it, the iris; and the vice depictions, the cornea. As if the message of this design were not clear enough—that our sins are always open to God's scrutiny, and that such scrutiny will determine our ultimate fate—an inscription in Gothic letters within the iris reads: "Beware, beware, God sees."[10]

More akin to the sin wheel on the church wall at Ingatestone in Essex than the illuminated diagram of Hugh's "five sevens," Bosch's painting illustrates the sins with genre scenes from daily life rather than allegorical figures. One of these scenes bears a marked similarity to the envy depiction from the Ingatestone wheel. In Bosch's painting, though, the scene is ascribed to avarice and not to envy: a seated judge is being approached by two petitioners—one, a wealthy man, accompanied by his lawyers; the other, to judge from his dress and demeanor, a humble peasant. The judge is using the long staff in his right hand to hold the latter off; yet, at the same time, he is reaching backhanded with his left to accept a sack of coins that the poor man has brought as the requisite bribe. Meanwhile, the wealthier man bends toward the judge in confidential conversation—and also holds his bulging money bag where it cannot help but be seen. If the point of the Ingatestone painting was to critique the envious motives that prompt neighbors to haul one another into court, the point in Bosch's vignette is to expose the greedy motives that corrupt those who are supposed to be enacting justice there.

Envy, however, is right next door in Bosch: avarice and envy appear on the table as scenes that could almost be taking place simultaneously in the same market town. The *Invidia* vignette is psychologically elaborate, with crisscrossing currents of envy connecting the multiple characters. (See Figure 6 on p. 44.) There are eight of them in all: six human and two canine—and the importance of the two dogs, front and center, should not be overlooked. They act out, in miniature, the focal drama of envy: with bones on the ground between them, nevertheless one of them looks up, barking, at a larger bone being held nonchalantly by one of the human figures. Meanwhile the other dog gives its companion a sidelong glance, no doubt wondering if that noisy mutt is going to get preferential treatment. In the medieval bestiary tradition, so influential for the symbolism of Bosch and others, dogs had a double-sided reputation: while they were occasionally praised for their intelligence and loyalty, they were also deplored as greedy and unprincipled scavengers. Even today, to say that someone has "gone to the dogs" is scarcely flattering in its implications.

Meanwhile, back in Bosch's vignette of envy, the human characters are engaging in their own share of sidelong glances. The central action is taking place at a customs house on the edge of a market town, where the tax collector is receiving a street tax from passers-by. Or, more accurately, his attractive daughter is stationed at the booth's open window, where she is collecting payment (with interest, so to speak) from a wealthy gentleman who is clearly captivated by her charms. In a sense, then, the publican is metaphorically dangling his daughter in front of moneyed citizens in the same way he literally dangles a large bone over the heads of the two rival dogs. And, just as one dog barks to attract attention and the other watches with envious suspicion, so a friend of the wealthy gentleman at the payment window regards with chagrin the social success of his companion.

Thus far, then, we can discern "evil eye" currents crossing between two dogs and two human friends. But this only begins to unravel the dynamics of this visual psychodrama. Further, the facial expression of the tax collector betrays some sneering resentment toward the elegant gentleman he is nonetheless allowing to banter with his daughter. Then,

Figure 6. Detail view of *Envy* (*Invidia*), from *The Table of Wisdom*. Source: Prado Museum. Used under Creative Commons Attribution/Share-Alike License: https://commons.wikimedia.org/wiki/File:Jheronimus_Bosch_Table_of_the_Mortal_Sins _(Invidia)2.jpg.

too, the tax collector's wife, behind his left shoulder, surveys the whole scene with distaste. Is hers the envy of a woman, past her prime, for her daughter, in the bloom of youth? the envy of the wife of a publican for her daughter's prospects of a marriage above her station? the envy of a working woman for the elegant attire and manners of the leisured class? Any or all could be the case.

Last but not least, off to the far right of the scene, almost as if wandering into the neighboring vignette (appropriately enough, on the sin of anger), staggers a peasant in a worn-out jerkin and breeches he has almost outgrown. He is bent almost double beneath the load of a heavy malt sack. If we look closely at this poor fellow, between the crook of his bent elbow and the weight of the burden he is toting, we can see him peering backward, hostility in his eyes, at the well-dressed chap to the right of the tax booth, who has nothing heavier to bear (so to speak) than the falcon perched on his arm. Even the angle of the peasant's body tells a story, as it curves around identically to that of the second dog, peering over its shoulder at its yapping rival.

Bosch entangles us in a veritable web of malicious glaring. Then, just in case his pointed satire has not yet fully persuaded us of the error of our own envious ways, he points out the gravity of the vice again in the vignette of hell, situated in the left-hand corner of the *Table of Wisdom*, immediately below the scene we have just been describing. This painting of hell, while less stylistically accomplished than the infernos that characterize his later work, nonetheless gives glimpses of the fascination with bizarre, demonic figures that make Bosch seem so eerily surrealist to modern viewers. In the hell medallion, we once again meet the seven deadly sins, in another kind of miniature sin wheel. But in this illustration of the "last things," the vices are no longer being realistically enacted. Rather, they are being punished in allegorical fashion, with the kind of *contrapasso*—or "punishment fitting the crime"—that Dante exemplified in his *Divine Comedy* nearly two hundred years earlier (and that we will encounter in our next chapter). The envious meet their fate at roughly twelve o'clock on the smaller wheel. To those who have paid attention to Bosch's imagery in the larger genre scene, the form of their punishment should come as no surprise: they are being torn apart by dogs. Once willing to destroy their neighbors over matters of no more ultimate significance than bones, in their final destiny they are reduced to being little more than bones themselves.

Turkeys, Shoes, and Pieter Bruegel

In the 1550s, some thirty years after his death, a Bosch revival occurred in Antwerp.[11] The work of Pieter Bruegel the Elder contributed to this revival. Bosch-influenced images are prominent in his engravings of the seven deadly sins. Other symbols, by now familiar to us, crowd into in his depiction of envy. (See Figure 7.) Again we find dogs, front and center, fighting over a bone. Dame Envy, again an allegorized female figure, stands behind the dogs, eating her heart out.

A Flemish proverb at the bottom of the page makes a parallel point: "Envy, endless death and cruel sickness . . . is a self-devouring beast." xFurther developing this maxim is one especially sobering figure. To the viewer's left from Dame Envy, a man lies on his back in a boat, with one skeletal leg draped over the side. But the man's swollen torso has

Figure 7. Pieter Bruegel, *Envy.* Source: Kupferstich, Herrausgeber: Hieronymus Cock. Bibliothèque Royale, Cabinet Estampes, Brüssel. Used under Creative Commons Attribution/ Share-Alike License: http://commons.wikimedia.org/wiki/File:Brueghel _-_Sieben_Laster_-_Invidia.jpg.

been completely consumed, and from its gaping hole a thicket of dry branches emerges. On a platter resting on a cloth below the man's chin lies a rounded object, which might be an apple—or might be his heart. Bruegel anticipates T. S. Elliot by several centuries with his image of "the hollow man"—but the source of this one's hollowness is (or was) his own corrosive envy.

Themes of hollowness and consumption appear elsewhere in Bruegel's engraving as well. Immediately behind Dame Envy, to the viewer's right, leans the trunk of a dead and hollowed-out tree. Behind that stands a furnace, its mouth gaping open and smoke from inner flames billowing outward. A demon clambers through the doorway to usher inside a naked sinner being hauled up for his punishment. And in the very back of the drawing, on the far left, the open mouth of a volcano belches fire.

A further motif curiously appears throughout the Bruegel drawing. Everywhere we look, we see *shoes*: a winged fish-monster in the lower left corner stuffs a shoe into his mouth; next to him, a sad old woman, a shoe perched on her head, sits in a basket from which she displays shoes that she is trying, with no luck, to sell. Meanwhile, across the page in the lower right-hand corner, naked sinners stand in a row, awaiting their turn to have shoes—all the same shape and size—forced on their feet by a far-busier shopkeeper, assisted by a wimpled demon. In front of this busier shop stands a bare tree, decorated by two boots stuck onto its branches. And to the back right, a giant's two legs flail out of the top of a broken money pot into which he has been upended, as an army approaches with staves, ladders, and lassoes to rob him of his hip boots. One of these, in fact, has already been appropriated; the other is pierced with an arrow and will doubtless soon become another trophy of war. The point is that envy always *longs to be in someone else's shoes*. Shoes, indeed, are a clear indication of one's social *standing*. (In English, we even contrast the "well-heeled" and those "down at the heels.") But regardless of jockeying for wealth or position in this life, in the life hereafter, the envious will all be shod with the same size—whether the shoe fits them comfortably or not.

One more initially puzzling image from the Bruegel drawing of envy deserves our attention: a turkey. To understand it, we are helped by looking at Bruegel's engraving for the related sin of pride. There, the featured animal is a peacock with its tail feathers puffed out in elaborate display, mimicking the flared skirt of his mirror-gazing Mistress Pride's high fashion attire. In contrast, Dame Envy has a turkey whose tail feathers fan out, but not in shimmering blue-green splendor. Surely this drab, brown bird envies its more stunning fellow creature. Just in case we might miss the point of this contrast, Bruegel strews peacock feathers around his envy engraving, too, with their figurative "eyes" wide open.

Significant implications also emerge from comparing Bruegel's engraving of envy with his depiction of love that—as in Giotto—appears as the directly contrasting virtue. Love has her own companion animal: a pelican perched atop her head, bending to pierce itself in the breast so that it can feed its young with its body and blood—an act which, for the medieval bestiary tradition, likened the pelican to Christ. Notable as well is the Lady's own gesture: like Giotto's figure of love, she does not eat her heart out but rather gives it away.

Luca Penni

A native Florentine, like Giotto; a social critic, like Bosch; and a contemporary of the elder Bruegel, Luca Penni was employed in the famous School of Fontainebleau at the court of Francis I. The work of Penni that concerns us here is a set of eight drawings titled "Justice and the Seven Deadly Sins."[12] Etched by engraver Léon Davent in the mid-sixteenth century, these works differ in style from anything we have yet seen. Yet, their overall format remains strikingly familiar: four corner vignettes or *tondi*, surrounding a central scene—though this scene appears in a slightly flattened oval rather than in a perfectly spherical "sin wheel." Almost every motif we have considered thus far is repeated somewhere in Penni's five scenes of envy.

The central image is the most complex. Again, it features an allegorized Dame Envy, but she no longer stands squarely front and center. Rather, she twists around the right-hand margin of the drawing. She is hideous: nude and cadaverous, with shriveled breasts that hang like daggers pointing toward the flames of hell arising from the bottom of the scene. Flames also seem to shoot from her Medusa-like hair, illustrating that the fires of her torment come from within as well as without. In her muscular and defiant arms, she clutches the thunderbolts of Zeus, emblems of another's glory that she has tried to seize. In her mouth, she clutches—not surprisingly—a venomous snake. All around her, demonic figures twist and turn, tugging her down toward the figure of Cerberus, the three-headed dog of classical mythology who guards the entrance to the underworld. Meanwhile, around the left margin of the oval, more dogs appear in a scene of desolation, tearing at the remains of a carcass on a barren plateau.

The four surrounding *tondi* pick up on several of these familiar images, supplementing them with scenes from biblical narrative and classical lore. Biblical stories occupy the upper left and lower right-hand corners, the former of these depicting the well-known story of Cain and Abel. As in Giotto, Bosch, and Bruegel, fire forms a dominant motif: in the background, we see the flames from two altars, their smoke mingling around the top of the roundel. The lamb of Abel's preferred sacrifice—the provocation for this scene of deadly enmity between brothers—is still partially visible on the altar to the right. In front of it, Abel lies on the ground, one arm flung upward in pleading or futile self-defense. Cain towers above him, wielding a club, intent on bludgeoning his brother to death.

Enmity between brothers is the topic of the biblical scene in the lower right-hand corner as well. Here, the adolescent Joseph sleeps in the foreground, his body at a similar angle to the one sketched out by Abel in the preceding vignette. Behind Joseph, we see images of the dreams he will imprudently share with his brothers, predicting his eventual superiority: eleven sheaves of grain bow down before a twelfth, as his eleven brothers will eventually pay him court; farther back, at the summit of the scene, the sun, moon, and stars also appear to do him honor (see Gen. 37:5–10). Meanwhile, on an elevation to the rear—spatially analogous to the barren plateau of the central oval where wild dogs skulk over carrion—the envious brothers gather to plot their revenge, stark silhouettes against the night sky.

Of the two remaining *tondi*—those from classical sources, occupying the diagonally opposite corners—one is equally ominous, and one conveys a bit of comic relief. The ominous one, on the bottom left, repeats imagery of an erupting volcano that we also encountered in Bruegel: a hollow pit, consumed from within by raging passions that it spews onto anyone who crosses its path. Commentators attribute Penni's volcano image to lines from Sebastian Brant's 1494 work, *The Ship of Fools*: "When Envy gnaws with eager bite, / She eats herself alone for spite. / Etna consumed itself alone."[13] On either side of the volcano, we see a ship capsizing, dashing masts and bodies against the mountain's rocky base. This image, too, derives from Brant: "Dame Envy only laughs when she / Has sunk a foe's ship out at sea."[14] This single tragic scene thus alludes to both sides of the classical definition of envy: gnawing sadness at a rival's good fortune, and malicious glee when that fortune goes awry.

Comic relief intervenes in the vignette on the upper right. Penni again draws deliberate parallels in imagery. Just as the motif of self-consuming fire links Dame Envy's descent into hell with the sacrifices of Cain and Abel and the volcanic eruption of Mount Etna, now the image of dogs returns to link the upper-right roundel with the central scene. In the focal drama, dogs are greedy scavengers, picking flesh off the bones of the dead. The smaller vignette presents a more satirical comment on canine (read: human) behavior. Penni illustrates Aesop's famous fable of "The Ox and the Dog," a classically "telling tale" of spiteful motives (which we will visit again in our following chapter). In the fable, a dog curls up for its afternoon nap in the manger of an ox. When the ox returns to the barn for dinner, the dog barks ferociously, threatening to bite the ox anytime it approaches the manger. Backing away sadly, the ox concludes that while the dog has no appetite for straw, it still begrudges the fodder to one who truly needs it.

The fable is the source of our English-language expression, "a dog in the manger," used to indicate someone who does not really want a thing for herself yet cannot stand that anyone else should have it. The dynamic is an invidious one, based on what we might think of as *dogged* status comparisons, made worse by the defensive fear that someone somewhere might get one up on us.

In many ways, Penni offers a fitting summation for the history of "arresting images" of envy from the tradition of the seven deadly sins. In subsequent eras, the rubric of the sins lost popularity. In large part, this loss resulted from the growth of Protestantism, with its insistence that all sins are equally horrid in the sight of God. There were, of course, still artists who broached the topic: a set of drawings by Jacques Callot in the seventeenth century, for example, once again focused on the seven deadlies, but the images show us nothing more than a synthesis of time-honored themes. (See Figure 8.) Dame Envy, as in Penni's engraving, is a jarring combination of boniness and muscularity, and her hair streams behind her like so many serpents or flames; a demon hovers behind her head to the left, and a starving and barking dog serves as her companion; on her outstretched right arm, she carries a snake; with the other, she raises her own heart to her lips for a bitter bite. What Morton Bloomfield says about literature can thus be applied more broadly: after the sixteenth century, the concept of the seven deadly sins "was never again to occupy an important part in life and culture. The *tradition* of the Sins was dead; they no longer evolved; they no longer inspired great writing"—or great art of other genres, either.[15]

Figure 8. Jacques Callot, *Envy* (*Invidia*), Image AN118165001 © Trustees of the British Museum. Used by permission.

Last Laugh

When images of the seven deadlies do occasionally crop up in our day, they tend to be more comic than dramatic. Satiric humor has its precedents, as we have seen: the turkey that would be a peacock; the dog in the manger; the dishonest judge and litigious neighbors; the woman with a snake curling out from her mouth, turning to bite her in her own eye. Yet, with few exceptions, today's cartoonish approach seems to take envy far more lightly. I think, for example, of an item advertised in a novelty catalog I received not long ago: a plaque sporting three pink pigs and the caption, "Lord, if you won't make me skinny, please make my friends fat!"

Certain motifs remain constant nonetheless: envy and "going to the dogs," for example. A few years ago, a friend passed along a cartoon that had caught his eye once he learned of my research in this area. In the foreground of the drawing stands a large tree, with one particularly thick and jutting branch. A beagle hangs about four feet off the ground, her teeth clamped to the branch, her tail wagging madly. The caption reads: "With this stick, Pepper knew she'd be the envy of the other dogs."[16] At first glance, there is something cute about this picture. Pepper in her tail-wagging delight is more endearing than the dogs snarling at oxen, fighting for bones, or picking over carrion in the demon-infested worlds of Bosch, Bruegel, Penni, and Callot. The cartoon beagle's desire to provoke the envy of her peers is surely not a matter for serious moral concern. Why, for the moment, Pepper is not really even hurting herself by clinging to her prize.

Still, if we extrapolate beyond the picture, adding to it a significance that is probably not intended, we have to acknowledge that if this silly, stubborn dog cannot eventually open her mouth and let go of her obsession, she could well starve to death—a moral which begins to sound like something out of another Aesop's fable: to which, among other "telling tales" of envy, we turn in our next chapter.

Chapter Four

Telling Tales

Many hundreds of years ago, there lived a man who bore more physical resemblance to a troll than a human being—or so uncharitable people said. He was very short, with stubby arms and bandy legs growing out of a torso that protruded in a little potbelly. Wherever he went, people called him names like "Monkey" and "Turnip" because of his homely appearance. For the first years of his life, he suffered from such a severe speech impediment that he could respond to his tormenters only in gesture, which roused them to further laughter at his expense.

But then one day, as legend has it, this man performed a service for a priestess of Isis. The goddess was so grateful for his assistance that she decided not merely to restore his powers of speech. More than this, she gave him a beautiful voice and an enchanting wit, such that he became one of the most famous storytellers the world has ever known. The man's reputation, thus, has lived happily ever after. The man himself, however, met with a less happy fate. One day when he had traveled to a land governed by a less grateful deity than Isis, an angry mob accused him of blasphemy and hurled him off a cliff.[1] Human beings do not take kindly to having our foibles displayed—even by a funny-looking little man with a silver tongue.

We ended our previous chapter with an allusion to Aesop, and we begin here with the same legendary Greek storyteller. Over the twenty-six centuries since he lived, Aesop's name has become virtually synonymous with fables as a genre of satiric and instructive animal tales. Many of his teachings have entered the fabric of our language: "a wolf in sheep's clothing"; "don't count your chickens before they hatch"; "slow and steady wins the race." For generations, his tales—along with vivid stories from a variety of other sources—served as important tools for moral instruction. Such

53

stories get our attention, and once they have it, they show us vividly that choices have consequences—consequences for the lives of those around us, to be sure, but also consequences for the types of people we turn out to be: honorable or dishonorable, generous-spirited or petty. In a culture in which a dishonorable and petty emotion like envy has come to be trivialized, we would do well to listen.

Fables and Foibles

A thirsty fox sees a cluster of grapes hanging from a branch. He hurls himself into the air over and over again, exhausting himself in unsuccessful attempts to knock them down. Finally acknowledging defeat, he concludes that they were probably sour anyway. While not envy proper, the fox's attitude fits under the broader heading of Capital Envy. It comes closest to that sub-sin Gregory the Great would have called detraction or "belittling." If we cannot have for ourselves something we wanted, we demean its value instead.

Not exactly envy proper, either, is the attitude of the dog-in-the-manger we met in the work of Luca Penni toward the end of chapter 3. Technically, that snarling beast is more begrudging than envious: he does not so much want something for himself (the hay in the manger) as he spitefully wants someone else (the ox) *not* to have it. Another dog fable comes closer to envy proper—and closer as well to illustrating its possible costs. A dog is happily trotting across a bridge, a bone in her mouth, when she spies below her the reflection of a dog carrying a bone. Like the competitive canines in Bosch's painting, aroused by what looks like a meatier morsel, she opens her mouth to bark—and loses what she has. The fable prods us to ponder what we might be losing in our own lives as a result of energies wasted hankering after the goods of others.

Also directly confronting the costs of envy proper is a fable called "Avaricious and Envious"—unusual in featuring human rather than animal actors. Versions of this cautionary narrative appear in a number of sources: Aesop's tales, a medieval French romance, a fifteenth-century Jewish devotional work.[2] Depending on the source, two men (Mr. Avaricious and Mr. Envious) appear before Jupiter, St. Martin, or a noble king. The god/saint/king offers to grant each man a wish, but with a catch: whatever the man wishes for, his companion will get double. The greedy man asks for wealth and gets it—but is sickened to see twice as much bounty lavished on his neighbor. The envious man then ponders long and hard—and asks to have one eye plucked out. The two are blinded by their vices, literally.

One fable moves beyond illustrating consequences of envy and begins to suggest a cure. "The Ass and the Charger" tells of a donkey that envies a horse's more luxurious food and stall, until war breaks out and the horse is ridden into combat. Like numerous other teaching tales, the story points out how envy tends to overlook the complexities of others' lives. The Country Mouse envies the fine foods at the City Mouse's disposal, until realizing the perils of urban life. Damocles's friend envies the king his power, until realizing that the monarch is in constant danger from enemies plotting against him. The more fully we understand our neighbors' lives, the more we are inclined to empathy instead of envy.

Thanks to translators and traveling storytellers, such moral tales became well-known across medieval Europe so that they could be adapted to feature a local legend like St. Martin or to appear in the work of a court artist like Luca Penni. Preachers' handbooks, mentioned in chapter 3 as tools created to assist in teaching the mandated Christian education curriculum, gathered sermon illustrations from far and wide. Some handbook editors even mentioned "Esopus" by name and argued against purists who objected to the use of pagan sources. The English Dominican friar John Bromyard, for example, pointed out that a patient and physician do not quarrel over the land where a needed medicinal herb is grown.[3] The implication seems clear. If we are sickened by envy and if pagan gardens, like Aesop's, bloom with healing insights, the least we can do is swallow our pride and take our medicine.

The Gods Must Be Envious

Other pagan gardens, therefore, merit a visit in our tour of "telling tales." The earliest of the great tragic poets of Athens, Aeschylus, dealt with the envy of both gods and mortals in his trilogy known as the *Oresteia*. In the first play of the trilogy, for example, after King Agamemnon returns from a brutal conquest of the Trojans, the Chorus cautions him that traitors may pretend to rejoice at his safe arrival while secretly wishing him ill. The conquering hero is not surprised. He responds:

> In few men is it part of nature to respect
> a friend's prosperity without begrudging him,
> as envy's wicked poison settling to the heart
> piles up the pain in one sick with unhappiness,
> who, staggered under sufferings that are all his own
> winces again to the vision of a neighbor's bliss.[4]

Yet, even Agamemnon does not realize how truly he speaks. Ultimately, he has far more to worry about than the envy of a few begrudging subjects. His triumphant success has also risked provoking the envy of the gods. The Greek notion of nemesis, which we encountered in chapter 2, warned against rising too high or taking more than one's just portion. Agamemnon has already tempted fate by being a "plunderer of cities," a "towering mountain." To assure his destruction, his embittered wife (demonstrating her own malice and hatred, offshoots of envy) provokes him to tempt fate one final time. Clytemnestra has never forgiven her husband for sacrificing their virgin daughter to the gods in order to gain fair winds for his fleet to sail into battle. Adding further insult to her injury, he has now returned from battle with a new mistress in tow. Both zealous to avenge her daughter's murder and jealous of her husband's wandering affections, Clytemnestra knows exactly how to pique Agamemnon to the ultimate act of overreaching—one that will seal his fate as a victim of the envious gods.

She summons her handmaids to strew crimson tapestries over the ground on which Agamemnon walks from his chariot to the palace door. Initially, he resists:

> [Do] not with your spread cloths invite
> Envy of gods, for honors due to gods alone.
> I count it dangerous, being mortal, to set foot
> On rich embroidered silks.
> (ll. 921-924)[5]

But Clytemnestra eggs him on, knowing that her husband is not a humble man. Predictably, he succumbs. As he removes his shoes to cross the purple pathway customarily reserved for a deity, he murmurs: "Let no god's eyes of hatred strike me from afar" (l. 947). Fulfilling the prophecy of his fears, Clytemnestra follows him into the palace and stabs him to death as his just retribution. She manages to destroy not only Agamemnon's life but also his honor, making him appear at the last little more than a pompous, over-reaching fool. If we are initially put off by this Greek notion that "the gods" may be envious of our good fortune, our own reflexive superstitions bear examining. How often do we "knock on wood" to keep good luck from turning bad? Or deflect a compliment with the (often-false) modesty of "It's nothing, really," as if to conceal our fortune from the equalizing eyes of fate? One further significant lesson that comes down to us from Aeschylus is that *provocation* to envy—whether of gods or mortals—is as dangerous as envying itself. Perhaps we should ponder this the next time we are urged to buy some product so that we can become "the envy of our friends."

East of Eden

While Greek stories took their place in the dispensaries of medieval preachers intent on diagnosing and prescribing against envy, a far more common source for such tales was the Bible. No sooner have Adam and Eve been expelled from Eden than an envy-motivated fratricide occurs in the Cain and Abel story. In the age of the patriarchs and matriarchs, Sarai envies her maid Hagar, who bears Abraham a son, and so casts the concubine out into the desert (Gen. 16:6). The "Philistines" (as they are mistakenly called in Gen. 26) envy Isaac's flocks and herds and so, in a gesture typical of envy, they fill his wells with dirt—an act that does nothing to increase their well-being but merely expresses their spite. Jacob envies his brother Esau's birthright and finds ways to trick him out of it (Gen. 27). Leah envies Rachel's beauty while Rachel envies Leah's success in bearing sons (Gen. 30). Joseph's brothers envy his favored status with their father and plot to sell him into slavery, as Luca Penni's engraving depicted (Gen. 37). The stories go on and on, passing from the generations of the Old Testament into the generations of the New, until (as we saw implied in Giotto's fresco in the Scrovegni Chapel), the scribes and Pharisees conspire to execute Jesus "out of envy."

Any of these tales would be worth exploring at length, but one not yet mentioned especially invites our attention. Recorded in 1 Samuel, chapters 16–24 and 26–27, it concerns the painful love-hate relationship between David, shepherd son of Jesse, and Saul, king of Israel. The tale opens with Saul's tragic loss of divine favor: the Spirit of the Lord has departed from him and he is tormented by inner demons instead. In this vulnerable state, the king meets David: a young man so skillful on the lyre that his music is able to soothe the older man's mental anguish. Understandably, Saul comes to love David. He responds by making the son of Jesse his armor-bearer, granting him positions of military leadership, and taking the young man into his own household.

The military leadership, however, turns out to invite disaster. David, it seems, is too good for his own good: or at least, too good for Saul's comfort. The young man goes out to war and is successful wherever Saul sends him. He becomes a folk hero. On one victorious return from battle against the Philistines, women turn out in droves, dancing and singing: "Saul has slain his thousands, / and David his ten thousands" (1 Sam. 18:7). It is not music to soothe Saul's ravaged spirit. The king's envy is inflamed. The following line is telling: "So Saul eyed David from that day on" (18:8–9).

This is, of course, none other than the "evil eye" of envy, which we have encountered in so many prior contexts. But Saul's anguish is such that he is not content simply to "look daggers" at the young man he fears will rob him of his throne. Instead, Saul hurls literal spears at David, trying to pin the younger man to the wall. When the agile—and, no doubt, mystified—target of the king's rage successfully evades him, Saul moves to more devious measures: sending David out on the life-endangering mission of procuring two hundred Philistine foreskins as a marriage present; sending servants of the royal court to David's house to kill him, forcing the formerly favored young man into hiding and a life on the run.

The sordid story of Saul's envy continues as he chases David, or has him chased, across the kingdom. In the wilderness of En-gedi (24:1–3) or the wilderness of Ziph (26:1–4), depending on the narrator, pursuer and pursued ultimately come face-to-face, and the tables are turned in a dramatic climax. David has it in his power to murder Saul in a moment of vulnerability and so rid himself of the man whose maniacal envy is seeking his destruction. But David cannot, or will not, bring himself to do it. In both versions of the story, Saul—at least for a moment—comes to his right mind, recognizes David's greater mercy in sparing the king's life, and offers him a blessing. Yet in neither version of the story does the moment of reconciliation hold. David is left to go on the run once again, even to the land of the Philistines. Israel's bitterest enemies have become safer to David than his envious former sponsor and friend.

We learn three things from this story. First, no amount of power or privilege provides a guarantee against envy; even though Saul is the king of Israel and the most powerful man in the realm, he is still provoked to hostility by David's popularity, military prowess, and position of divine favor. Second, no matter how patient the envied person may be, she can do little to soothe the envier's torment; in fact, largesse may only make matters worse, because it points out another way in which the envied person is "bigger" and more to be resented. Third, while Saul's envy creates a serious problem for David, forcing him into life on the run, it is ultimately the greatest agony for Saul himself. East of Eden, exiled from the paradise of right relationships, our rivalries *eat our hearts out*, leaving us hollow inside.

To be faithful to the stories in 1 Samuel, however, we should note that Saul lost God's favor for a reason: he disobeyed a direct divine command.

In this detail, we find a key difference between the worldview of the Hebrew authors and that of the Greeks: a focus on the *jealousy* of an Almighty whose goal is to preserve the prerogative of absolute obedience from human creatures, in contrast to the *envy* of a pantheon of deities whose goal is to temper the presumption of overreaching mortals. The most significant distinguishing issue is the perception of the appropriate human "place." In the culture of Aeschylus, it is a place of *moderation*: exercising one's human gifts, to be sure, yet keeping them in balance, lest one overreach oneself and thereby endanger not only oneself but also the harmony of the whole community. The heedlessly pompous person stirs up social unrest. Thus, it is in a culture's best interest to have a mythos—in the instance of the Greeks, an image of the leveling hand of Nemesis—which serves to keep such pomposity in check.

In the culture of the Hebrews, by way of contrast, the human "place" is not so much one of moderation as one of *obedience*. As long as Yahweh is enthroned at the center of personal and communal life, human ambition poses no threat. We are, in fact, made in God's own image (Gen. 1:26), given prerogatives of vice-regency over the realm of creation. For Saul to be a powerful human ruler is not a problem, so long as he and his people remain faithful to Yahweh as King of kings. But the minute Saul thinks he can take matters into his own hands, choosing which of God's commandments to obey and which to ignore, he loses favor. *Not* that Yahweh is *envious* of Saul's accomplishments (even the idea is unthinkable in Hebrew terms). Rather, the Lord our God is a *jealous* God, before whom we shall have no other: including the seductive mini-god of our own self-will.

Metamorphoses

Where biblical authors show us the ravages of envy in the lives of historical figures (like Saul) or proto-historical ones (like Cain), authors of classical antiquity move beyond cautionary tales to offer accounts of heroic figures too large to experience this petty passion in any degree. One of the earliest examples appears in Xenophon's account of the life of Cyrus of Persia. According to legend, Cyrus's grandfather once organized a hunt for his grandson but ordered no one to catch anything until the young man had had his kill. Cyrus, however—to his grandfather's delight—laughingly refused this concession, instead reveling in the successes of others "without the least display of envy."[6] In a similar vein, Plutarch cites the generous example of Caesar, who ordered that the statues of his defeated rival Pompey be restored.[7] Such hearty heroes—thrilled by competition, passionate about excellence wherever it appears, whether in themselves or in others, and thereby immune to envy—remain attractive models for our moral instruction. We will seek more such models in our closing chapter.

Far less attractive, though equally influential in the canon of "telling tales" about envy, are images from Ovid's *Metamorphoses*. Like Aesop, Ovid surprisingly crops up in medieval preachers' handbooks. A legend of rival sisters, Aglauros and Herse (used by Dante to balance the rival brothers of the Cain/Abel story, as we will shortly see), becomes the occasion for a visit to the house of Dame Envy. Ovid's literary imagery clearly inspired the visual images from Giotto to Penni to Callot that we explored in chapter 3. When the visiting goddess Minerva arrives at Envy's home, located in a valley of thick fog where no sun ever shines, Envy must abandon the half-eaten snake carcasses, "the food of her venom," strewn about her on the floor. Watts's translation (lines 775–782) merits citing at length:

> A shriveled hag was she,
> with squinting eyes, that looked askance at all,
> black, rotting teeth, and bosom green with gall.
> No color in her cheeks, no smile she had,
> save when the sight of sorrow made her glad.
> As, vexed with cares, her sleepless eyes survey
> men faring well, she eats her heart away;
> and, poison-tongued, the self-tormenting shrew
> inflicts a rankling wound, and feels one too.[8]

Summoned to follow Minerva to the home of the rival sisters, the hag picks up her thorny staff and cloaks herself in the black cloud that is her constant companion. Wherever she passes, flowers die, grasses wither, and the tallest trees droop and languish. With each passing breath, she pollutes the air of homes, cities, and entire nations. (In our own day, we might even dare to suggest that this repulsive figure continues to destroy nations when they forget her hideous attributes and come to think of Envy as an appropriate name for a perfume, a marketing gimmick to use without thought of the consequences to our individual and communal health.)

Pardoner's and Parson's Tales

While some medieval priests might have been reluctant to caution against Envy by quoting from Ovid—the author of racy material like the

Amores—others, as we saw earlier in discussing Aesop, were open to any source of vivid examples. Itinerant marketplace preachers had to compete for attention with minstrels, jongleurs, and traveling players and were open to help in the form not only of catchy illustrations but also advice about voice, posture, gesture, and means to establish rapport with an audience.[9] In a work written during the heyday of the preaching handbooks, the Pardoner (or indulgence-seller) in Chaucer's *Canterbury Tales* reports on his own sermonizing technique:

> Well, then, I give examples thick and fast
> from bygone times, old stories from the past.
> A yokel mind loves stories from of old,
> being the kind it can repeat and hold.[10]

It is not coincidental that these cynical lines about "yokels" come from the *Pardoner* and not the *Parson* in the *Canterbury Tales*. While the Pardoner is game for any sales technique, the Parson wants no part in the tricks proposed by preaching manuals. The Parson is convinced that he has the pure wheat of gospel to share; why, then, should he sink to chaff? Thus, when called on as the last of the pilgrims from London to Canterbury to offer up his tale, he warns:

> You'll get no fable or romance from me,
> for Paul, in his Epistle to Timothy
> reproves all those who waive aside the truth
> for fables that are wretched and uncouth.[11]

He consents to speak, but not to tell tales—or even speak in rhyme. Rather, he will give an exhaustive prose discourse on all the branches and sub-branches of sin and repentance known to scholastic theology: a *parser's* more than a *parson's* recitation.

The Parson's organizing rubric, not surprisingly, is the seven deadly sins. While some critics view his sermon as a parody of the dullest preaching of his day, it provides us with one of the most comprehensive analyses of envy and the other "deadlies" to appear in medieval thought. We will not linger long over the minutiae of branches and sub-branches, but a sampling is instructive.

Chaucer and his Parson have done their homework. In speaking of the "foul sin of envy," they turn immediately to its classical definitions: "according to the word of the philosopher," envy is sorrow for others' prosperity; and "according to the word of Saint Augustine," it is sorrow for others' well-being and joy for others' harm.[12] Beyond these standard points, the Parson goes on to conclude that envy is "the worst sin there is," because while all sins oppose virtue in some sense, envy flatly opposes *all* virtue and *all* goodness; instead of rejoicing in the right, it finds *any* good belonging to its neighbor to be a potential source of misery. The "twigs" off this main branch of envy initially are those we have come to expect after Gregory the Great: sorrow for other people's prosperity; joy for their adversity; detraction (backbiting and belittling); grumbling (gossiping and complaining); and bitterness.

Beyond this typical vice tree, each individual offshoot in the Parson's analysis produces its own set of twigs. Grumbling, for example, has six subsidiaries:

> grumbling against God over complaints ranging from bad weather to bad luck;
>
> begrudging born of greed, resentful of the distribution of resources;
>
> self-righteous grumbling, critical of those we deem undeserving of their good fortune;
>
> gossiping to expose the weaknesses of others;
>
> speaking spitefully about others in secret, fearful of opposing them face-to-face;
>
> nursing rancor in the heart, out of anger or hate.

While the Parson may not entertain us with stories to illustrate the various vices on his list, we would not be hard-pressed to come up with tales from our own experience of persons—including ourselves—who behave in these keenly observed ways.

Pilgrimage

Given its markedly different flavor, scholars have debated the relationship of the Parson's Tale (which is not a tale at all) to the rest of Chaucer's Canterbury narrative. Was this dry prose sermon really the note on which the author intended to conclude his lively poetic work? The host of the band of pilgrims had another end in view: according to Harry Bailey, the inn keeper, the ultimate goal of the pilgrimage was to return to London from Canterbury, judge the various tales told en route, and then indulge in a victory celebration. From such a perspective, the Parson's catalog of sins and sub-sins does seem anticlimactic.

But there is a vision of pilgrimage, different from Harry Bailey's, by which the Parson clearly merits the last word. If life itself is a journey from earth to heaven, from sin to redemption, what better conclusion for the Canterbury pilgrims than a discourse on sin and virtue, confession and repentance? After all, if they—and we—truly take to heart this teaching from the Parson, the "end" of our travels becomes not just an evening's revelry in some tavern but an eternity's joy at the banquet of the Lamb.

This broader view of pilgrimage figures in another influential medieval work filled with drama involving the sins that jeopardize our quest for heaven: Guillaume de Deguileville's *Pilgrimage of Human Life*.[13] Deguileville uses a basic allegorical plot, later adapted by John Bunyan in *Pilgrim's Progress*: the author is embarked on a journey to the Holy City. En route, he is guided by the character Grace Dieu and protected by the staff of Hope as he encounters various figures that will hinder his progress. Foremost among these are the seven deadly sins, in whose features we see reflections of the art of the day as well as the literature of antiquity.

After an initial skirmish with Sloth, the pilgrim meets the sins—again personified as female—in their standard Gregorian order. Pride, admiring herself in her mirror, appears at the head of the pack, followed closely by her daughter Envy, whose unholy father was Satan himself. As in so many interpretations connecting envy with the "evil eye," Deguileville's hag looks daggers at the Pilgrim—literally. Two venomous spears emerge from her eye sockets, enabling her to poison others with a glance. One of these spears is named Anger at a neighbor's joy; the other is named Joy at others' misfortune. Adding familiar biblical images to this classical definition, the crone explains that with the first, the spear of fury at another's good fortune, Saul struck at David, enraged that the shepherd boy had grown more popular than he; and with the second, Jesus was pierced by those who took malicious pleasure in mocking him at his crucifixion.

In her assault on the Pilgrim, Envy is accompanied by her two daughters, Treachery and Detraction. The former carries a mask behind which she conceals her ugly intentions, and a box of ointment or "soft, oily words" with which she anoints her adversaries before stabbing them with a hidden weapon. She is the "scorpion that stings from behind" and the "adder that lurks in the grass," the "willow in leaf, clothed in beautiful foliage but all hollow or full of worms inside."

Detraction, on the other hand, makes no attempt to conceal her malice. She lunges at the Pilgrim, "barking and gnawing" and threatening to eat him alive. The most vicious of the pack of dogs that have served as icons of envy over the ages, she brags, "You never in your life saw a mastiff or a bitch in a butcher shop that eats raw flesh as ferociously as I do." Yet, she admits she would rather devour carrion or rotted food than fresh—and to this end, she will slander and defame good people until they are foul enough for her to consume. "I do not have to go far if I want to find rottenness," she boasts; "I have the tools to make it in my mouth." In addition to the weapon of her sharp and defiling tongue, she carries a spear on which are impaled the ears of all those who listen to her gossip and slander—an image that calls to mind the misshapen ears on the crone of Envy in Giotto's fresco, even as Treachery's earlier talk of adders and venom calls to mind the snake emerging from this same figure's mouth and turning to bite her in the eye.

Envy, Treachery, and Detraction all take a run at the Pilgrim, striking him with lances, spears, and daggers; biting and gnawing on his flesh; anointing him with ointment; and then stabbing him in the belly with a knife. They are confident that he will not escape their assaults, "unless he has an excellent physician." But of course he does have the greatest physician of all on his side. The protection of Christ is guaranteed him, both by the sacraments that sealed him before his journey and by the staff of Hope to which he firmly clings.

Purgation

Better known than this dramatic work by Deguileville, the most famous piece of pilgrimage literature to emerge out of the century of Chaucer and Giotto is the *Divine Comedy* of Dante Alighieri. Again, the author-as-pilgrim embarks on a journey: this time, through all the levels of hell and purgatory in order to reach paradise and an ecstatic vision of God. Although some authors have attempted to locate the seven deadly sins in the first volume of Dante's trilogy, the *Inferno*, in actuality it is the *Purgatorio* for which this list provides the organizing scheme. Each sin is purged on a successive tier or cornice of Mount Purgatory. The pattern is always the same: repentant souls are confronted with examples of the vice in question to serve as warnings and with examples of its contrary virtue to offer inspiration; they are cleansed by *contrapasso*, a purgation distinctively fitted to their prior crime; they sing a hymn and receive a Beatitude expressive of the newness of life to which they aspire. In good Gregorian order, pride is the first sin to be addressed. As always, envy comes second.

When Dante and his guide Virgil first emerge onto the cornice of envy, they are shocked by its barrenness: in contrast to the pomp and splendor of pride just below, envy seems petty and empty. All they see is blue-black (*livido*) stone, the color of a bruise. It is worth noting that the Latin roots for the Italian word *livido*—the noun *livor* and its adjective form *lividus*—refer either literally to this blue-black color or metaphorically to envy and spite: emotions that bruise the spirit and discolor the whole world of those who suffer from them. Examples of the virtues opposite to envy take the form of disembodied voices that whirl around the mountain past the pilgrim and his guide. The most powerful of these is the voice of Christ himself, crying: "Love those who have done you harm" (Canto XIII). The Suffering Servant who was given up to crucifixion "out of envy" still loved his enemies enough to forgive them for what they did.

No sooner have the voices of virtue flown past than Dante happens upon the ranks of the penitent enviers. Dressed in haircloth the same color as the stone of the mountain, they are crowded along its bank, leaning against one another's shoulders for support—an acknowledgment of interdependence that none of them would have willingly made during their competitive lives. In one of the most "arresting images" of the repertoire of portrayals of envy, Dante has their eyelids pierced with iron wire and stitched shut. Thus, people who once sinned with their eyes, blinded to true goodness and casting evil glances at those deemed more fortunate, now are punished at the site (or literally, the "sight") of their crime.

Dante hears the confessions of former residents of Florence who admit to how "livid" they became at the good fortune of others and how pleased to see those fortunes turn sour. In particular, they point to political rivalries that consumed their lives on earth. Now that they are being purged of pettiness, they mourn the factionalism that is tearing their earthly homeland apart. At last they have realized that "we are all citizens of one true city." Within this political message about the costly hostilities involving the city-states of his day, Dante offers us a deeper theological point: the truest cure for envy lies in the enlargement of our loves, the expansion of our horizons, until we come to see our neighbors' goods and griefs as belonging to us as well.

Dante the pilgrim and we, his traveling companions, will learn more of this lesson in a moment. But suddenly, the air around us is split by two thunderous cries. This time, the disembodied voices remind us of the seriousness of the vice. First, we hear from Cain, who killed his own brother out of envy and thereafter lived in terror that all earthly contacts would be similarly death-dealing. Second, we hear from Aglauros, the envious sister who met with Dame Envy in Ovid's *Metamorphoses*. Thus we encounter a biblical and a classical source of the ravages wrought by hatred of brother and hatred of sister—rubrics which ultimately encompass *all* forms of envious sinning.

Before we leave the cornice of envy, Dante takes us through another lesson about its remedies. We should love as Christ loves, he insists; we should see ourselves as citizens of a common city, sisters and brothers of all. And we should learn what goals are truly worth pursuing. As long as we set our sights on worldly goods that are in fixed supply, one person's possessions will diminish what is available for others. But if we shift our sights to long instead for spiritual goods, then the more our neighbors possess, the more we enjoy as well. Joy, peace, charity, hope: such "fruits of the Spirit" are not divided but *multiplied* by being shared.

As if to drive home this point about the remedial virtue of expansive love, Dante uses the word *caritas* four times in the three cantos devoted to envy and nowhere else in the entire *Purgatorio*.[14] Further sealing the message about generosity of spirit, the angel at the stairway leading out of the cornice of envy cries out: "Blessed are the merciful!" Meanwhile, the repentant sinners whom Dante leaves behind demonstrate their progress in celebrating rather than begrudging the victory of another. As he journeys beyond them toward paradise, they sing to him with genuine gladness: "Rejoice, you who have won!"

Pageants

In a letter to a friend, Dante acknowledged that he wrote the *Divine Comedy* to serve as a kind of guide, to help others move "from a state of misery . . . toward a state of happiness."[15] What better motive for the creator of any "telling tale"—or "arresting image," for that matter—than a desire to illustrate ways to be and *not* to be, in words and pictures vivid enough to inspire our pursuit of genuine flourishing?

Such a motive lies behind a final genre of tales in the medieval Christian repertoire of works on the deadly sins in general, and the sin of Capital Envy in particular. The *pageant* narrative, in fact, constitutes a sort of pilgrimage-in-reverse: instead of questing people setting out on a journey and encountering each of the allegorized sins in turn, here the human spectators stay in one place while the sins pass in review before their eyes. Such pageant scenes show the influence of morality plays with their personified figures of virtue and vice, and of Corpus Christi parades, hugely popular in the medieval world from the festival's beginning in 1264 until the Protestant Reformation.

Perhaps the most famous of the literary pageant scenes occurs in William Langland's fourteenth-century *Piers Plowman*, in an episode known as "The Shriving of the Seven Deadly Sins."[16] After a stirring call to repentance, each of the sins steps forward in turn to confess its hideous nature. Following the customary Gregorian order, *Pride* comes first. Then, after a hasty interlude on *Lecherie* or Lust, *Envy* moves center stage. Langland's Envy is in the school of Hieronymus Bosch's vignettes from daily life, personified not as an allegorized female but as a surly male. Still, he has many features in common with the allegorical tradition. He carries a knife at his side, ready to stab anyone who annoys him— preferably in the back. Each word he speaks is "of an adder's tongue." His chief livelihood is "backbiting" and "bearing false witness."

In fact, no sooner does Envy step forward, allegedly to confess his misdeeds, than he begins cursing his enemies. He seizes the opportunity to complain about his neighbor's new coat, which he wishes he had instead. Repentance warns Envy that if he wishes to be forgiven, he must admit that he is sorry. Indeed, Envy replies, he is seldom anything but sorry; he is so sorry that he is wasting away, consumed by his own bile, unable to eat. As it turns out, though, he is sorrier for *himself* than for his sins. He feels, he says, "as loveless as a lousy [meaning louse-infested] dog."

He snarls like one, too. Given such hostility, it makes sense that envy keeps close company with anger in lists of the deadly sins. Following the order established by Gregory I, Dante makes envy the second sin to be redeemed on Mount Purgatory—just after pride and just before wrath. Likewise, in Deguileville's *Pilgrimage* or in Langland's *Piers Plowman*, anger storms onto the scene on envy's very heels. The same order holds in yet another tale of the ravages of envy: the pageant of the deadly sins in Edmund Spenser's sixteenth-century *Faerie Queene*.

Roughly two hundred years later than the other texts we have been exploring for the past several pages, roughly contemporary with Luca Penni, Spenser's work forms a bridge between medieval and Renaissance sensibilities. Unlike his Catholic predecessors—Dante, Deguileville, and Langland—Spenser wrote in the newly Protestant culture of Elizabethan England. Yet he was not willing to forego the rich imagery housed in the Catholic tradition of the seven sins—even if he used that very imagery to criticize the Roman church.

In one layer of interpretation, the Redcrosse Knight, hero of the *Faerie Queene*, personifies the country of England. When the story opens, he is in company of Lady Una—allegorically, the one true church (for Spenser, the Church of England, presided over by Elizabeth I, the Virgin

Queen). Yet, early on he is deceived into abandoning his lady, just as England had abandoned the Protestant Reformation during the turbulent years between the death of Henry VIII and Elizabeth's accession. Redcrosse succumbs to the wiles of Lady Duessa—the personification of duplicity (also known as "Fidessa," thus representing the "bad faith" of allegedly corrupt Catholicism). While he is in the throes of his infatuation with Duessa/Fidessa, Redcrosse takes refuge in the House of Pride, where Queen Lucifera and her attendants, the deadly sins, parade before his eyes.[17]

"Proud Lucifera" rides in a glittering coach, drawn by "six unequal beasts" on which her sage counselors and motley ministers ride (a further "arresting image" of how sins tend to travel in packs rather than individually). These six are none other than the remaining capital sins. Theirs is no orderly processional, however, with the sins marching single file or two by two. Rather, they jostle along six abreast, each of their beasts tugging for supremacy and trying to crowd the others out of the way.

Envy rides a ravenous wolf: we note awareness of this sin's devouring hungers once more. In disgusting reinforcement of the theme, Envy holds in his mouth a venomous toad, which he chews with such vigorous tooth-gnashing that the poison gushes down his face. In his breast, he bears a snake with a mortal sting. Inwardly, he "chaw[s] his own maw"— which we, as students of the tradition, might now liberally translate as "he eats his own heart out." But Envy is not content simply to *chew* venom; he must *spew* it as well. So sickened is he by any signs of superiority in others, that he cannot celebrate their good works; rather, he misrepresents and maligns them. His "leprous mouth" speaks shriveling words, turning every good to bad.

Like Chaucer's Parson, Spenser has done his homework—and so his portrait gives a fitting summation of the expected imagery of envy: the dog (or in this case, wolf); the vipers and venom; the cavernous and corrosive hungers of the heart. As we have come to expect, "the eyes have it" in the *Faerie Queene*'s climactic depiction of this deadly vice as well. Capital Envy is swathed in a multicolored silk cloth coat, "painted full of eyes."

Paradigms Lost

As the pageant of Lucifera and the Deadly Sins parades forth, huge crowds throng the way, shouting with joy at the gruesome sight. Spenser's satire of the corruption in both the secular and ecclesial cultures of his day is thick. Contrast this with the practitioners of the "triumphant therapeutic" in our own day, who counsel us that envy is perfectly normal and nothing to feel bad about.

Of course, Spenser is too keen a moralist to let his parading vices simply ride off into the sunset. Rather, they enjoy a few moments in the fresh air—and then turn around and head straight back to the palace, where they remain to wreak havoc on the governance of daily affairs. However, with the *Faerie Queene*, the motif of the seven deadly sins itself does begin its journey into the sunset, fading from popularity as a serious model for understanding the life of virtue and vice. The Protestant reformers looked askance at the tradition, seeing it as part of the penitential apparatus of the Roman church whose excesses they, along with Spenser, deplored: the buying and selling of indulgences (from unscrupulous hawkers, like Chaucer's Pardoner); the tedious delineation of sins and sub-sins (like the sermon by Chaucer's Parson), neglecting the one sin that truly matters—the failure to give a rightfully *jealous* God our exclusive love and obedience.

One last literary gasp does appear in Christopher Marlowe's *Doctor Faustus*—one last pageant of the seven deadly sins, although it is more a parody of earlier pageants that had aimed at shaping repentance in the reader. Marlowe's play-within-a-play seems intended solely for comic relief. Faustus, having made his pact with the devil, is beginning to waver. Is it too late to repent and be saved from damnation? To distract him from such questions, Beelzebub offers a little light entertainment: a parade of the seven deadly sins. Faustus agrees.

In they march.[18] Most of the elaborate iconography has gone. Envy, again positioned near Wrath, has little to say for himself, a mere seven sentences. He is "lean from seeing others eat"—a line reminiscent of all those envious figures we have observed who waste away, consumed with longing for that which is not theirs. Only if all the rest of the world suffered a famine would he grow fat with joy at their misfortune. One of the lines that Marlowe gives to Envy is a newcomer to the repertoire, but quickly becomes a classic: "I cannot read and therefore wish all books burned." Here is Aesop's dog-in-the-manger, neatly adapted from an agricultural to a post-Gutenberg context.

But that is it. To be sure, since Marlowe's day great literature has continued to concern itself with the ravages of envy, but no more do we get the concentrated treatment that comes with the cardinal sins tradition. We would have to read hundreds of pages of Shakespeare or Steinbeck, Eliot or Austen, to get the equivalent of one iconic paragraph from *Piers Plowman* or any of the other "telling tales" we have been exploring through this chapter. These tales were told with the express intent of providing memorable moral instruction in compressed enough form that even a largely preliterate audience could "get the picture." From the 1600s forward, the paradigms were lost. The deadlies were dulled, except, of course, as they remain in the secret recesses of our lives.

Chapter Five

Spoiled Psyches

Mirror, mirror on the wall, who's the fairest of them all? Echoes of this familiar question follow us across a bridge from historical "telling tales" of envy to contemporary psychological analyses of the experience. Perhaps we heard the story of Snow White when we were growing up, or saw the animated Disney version, or encountered the narrative later in life with children of our own. But now, having more fully explored the deadly sins tradition, we should understand the question afresh. Recognizing the mirror as part of the traditional iconography of pride, we are instantly alerted to the fact that the wicked queen's pride will be injured when she learns of a rival to her beauty.

Iconography of envy illumines other details of the story. When the queen discovers that her stepdaughter has grown more beautiful than she, the envious older woman instructs a huntsman to take the child into the forest, kill her, and bring back the young girl's bodily organs for the queen to devour. Why make such a gruesome request, except that the queen desires to *eat someone else's heart out* rather than her own? Later in the story, when Snow White has escaped her intended death and gone to live among the seven dwarfs, the queen discovers her hiding place and comes in disguise to visit, intent on killing her with a poisoned apple. This symbol is so close in appearance to what the wicked woman would *rather* have the more beautiful stepdaughter eat—namely her own heart—that in artistic renderings of envy through the ages, we often cannot tell whether it is a heart or an apple that the envious person is consuming.

In the world of the fairy tale, however, the apple—or the attempted provocation to envy—sticks in the virtuous Snow White's craw. It chokes her, such that she lies in a deathly sleep for many years. When

71

the poisoned bite is finally dislodged, she is restored to live happily ever after. Not so, the wicked queen. As the Grimm brothers tell the story, the envious stepmother meets an unhappy, if oddly appropriate, fate. At a banquet in Snow White's honor, the vengeful old woman is forced to don iron slippers that have been heated red-hot in a fire and to dance until she drops down dead. Such is the severe penalty for having wanted so desperately to be in someone else's shoes.

This shoe motif, which appeared so puzzling when we first saw it in Bruegel's engraving of envy, now awakens a nod of recognition. We encounter the motif in another classic story of envy, Cinderella. What more graphic representation could there be of the envious stepsisters' desire to be in their lovelier sibling's shoes than the fact that they are willing to butcher themselves to make her footwear fit? In an effort to cram their appendages into the coveted slipper, one sister hacks off her toe and the other mutilates her heel. Envy, as we have seen repeatedly, is the source of its own misery. Further driving home the moral that envious people come to painful ends, the fairy tale sees to it that the wicked stepsisters are doubly afflicted. On their way to Cinderella's wedding with Prince Charming, the stepsisters' eyes are pecked out by avenging pigeons. Like Dame Envy in Giotto's Scrovegni Chapel fresco or the envious penitents of Dante's *Purgatorio*, those who plague others with the evil eye of envy are ultimately punished at the site (or sight) of their malevolence.

Snow White's Stepmother

Like the teaching tales of the deadly sins tradition, fairy tales carry their meanings in compact packages. Their plots are basic and generic; their characters are clearly drawn. Good and evil are both present, but personified in ways that leave no doubt as to which is which. This absence of ambiguity is especially helpful for children, who are just embarking on the process of learning to make the distinctions that will eventually form their systems of value. Fairy tales dramatize psychological issues that young people will face as their lives unfold, and they reinforce a foundational hope that evil will be punished and good will triumph to "live happily ever after."

In his book *The Uses of Enchantment*, Freudian analyst Bruno Bettelheim discusses in detail the ways childhood conflicts are enacted and resolved in fairy tales.[1] While "Cinderella," which we shall address in a moment, deals directly with the dangers of envying and being envied by siblings, "Snow White" is more roundabout in addressing the Oedipal dangers of being envied by our elders. Indeed, it seems particularly apt to talk about Oedipal dilemmas in the context of "Snow White," since Oedipus himself was a child taken out into the forest to die, lest he grow to be too much of a rival for his father.

Clearly, the central drama in the Snow White story is played out between the wicked queen of "Mirror, mirror" fame and her beautiful stepdaughter. If we share Bettelheim's Freudian perspective, we see in this drama some of the young child's mingled desire and fear of taking the place of the same-sexed parent in the affections of the parent of the opposite sex. Snow White stands for any child caught up in a rivalry with her elders and afraid of the consequences. Just as a child may long to be rid of a parent with whom competing (and inevitably losing) seems unbearable, so she may project onto a parent—or, more safely in the fairy tale world, a *step*parent—the longing to be rid of potentially competitive offspring. Hence, the numbers of wicked stepmothers in the fairy tale world who devise plots to harm or destroy their stepchildren (think of "Hansel and Gretel," for another example). Fortunately for the sake of the child's secure psychological development, this longing to eliminate younger rivals is thwarted in the tales. Children sent into the woods to be lost or killed inevitably find their way back out alive. Stepparents who attempt to do away with their young are outwitted and made to pay. Envy gets exposed to the light where it can be seen and handled, but it does not win.

Beyond the Oedipal drama of the young child, the Snow White story also depicts elements of a conflict between older and younger generations. Unfortunately for children's secure psychological development, some parents are so self-involved that they cannot stand to see their offspring grow into independent individuals. Initially, they want their children to remain forever as extensions of themselves (think of Wanda Holloway, who sought to fulfill her frustrated ambitions through her daughter's success as a cheerleader). Once the child establishes independence, the parent may get caught up in competing *with* rather *through* the younger one's accomplishments: the father *has* to win at video games; the mother cannot stand for her daughter to be thinner than she. Such battles intensify at adolescence, when the child's chances for actual victories expand. Indeed, in an era of frequent divorce when many mothers and fathers find themselves newly single, the likelihood increases that some will vie with their teenage children for success in dating. The narcissistic and immature modern-day stepmother of Snow White, for example, will feel consumed with envy to witness her daughter's effortless beauty while she herself fights the physical alterations of aging.

Nor is it simply parents or stepparents who are likely to experience the rage of Snow White's wicked queen. Junior faculty members, junior partners in a law firm, junior executives in a business office: all these have occasion to suffer effects of the "Mirror, mirror on the wall" syndrome. Who's the brightest of them all, the strongest, the quickest, the most energetic and resourceful? When the answer to the old guard comes back "not you anymore, but Junior there," sometimes the best that "Junior" can hope for is to be offered the poisoned apple of patronizing praise: "Yes, well, I'm sure that does seem like a good idea to you, but when you've had as much experience as I, you'll know better." In turn, "Junior" may feel the need to "lie low" (symbolically, to sleep for a hundred years) until the danger passes.[2] Where *patronizing* supplants *patronage* in the attitude of the older generation toward the younger, both jealousy and envy are making themselves felt: "jealousy," as senior persons desire to keep their present status from being taken away; "envy," as they simultaneously long for and resent the superior attributes of the up-and-coming. Helmut Schoeck speculates that much resistance to innovation is born of such intergenerational envy.[3] Mark Gillman has written an entire book on *Envy as a Retarding Force in Science*, describing ways in which old guard authorities have thrown roadblocks into the path of such innovators as Galileo, Darwin, and William Morton (the developer of ether anesthesia).[4] Some anthropologists posit that the painful elements in so many puberty rites—scarring and circumcision, or in our own culture, the far milder "birthday spanking"—act as a sop to the ego of older generations, compensating for their pain at being rivaled and eventually replaced.[5] Existential psychologist Adrian van Kaam further hypothesizes that envy was the force behind the symbolic assassination of a king or other outstanding individual, who was offered in ancient cultures as a sacrifice to the gods.[6] In this light, we might think anew about the action of the chief priests who offered Jesus of Nazareth up to crucifixion "out of envy" (Matt. 27:18; Mark 15:10 RSV).

Cinderella's Siblings: A Freudian Perspective

If these psychological and anthropological analyses are right, at certain moments in our lives, all of us are Snow White, victimized by the envy of our elders, just as all of us become the wicked queen, threatened by younger competitors for our status and prestige. But in the consumer culture that has been growing in the United States since the early decades of the twentieth century, we may be even more plagued by envy directed at nearer neighbors, the proverbial Joneses with whom we are trying to keep up. Such "sibling" rivalries put us squarely in league with Cinderella and her stepsisters.

Even cultures less afflicted by sibling striving than our own have found rich veins of meaning in the Cinderella story. Its appeal has something to do with the rags-to-riches motif of the successful underdog as well as the universality of psychological tensions between peers, whether children of the same parents or members of some other common grouping. Many commentators have pointed out that the Cinderella story is both the oldest and the best-loved of all fairy tales, with variants dating as far back as the ninth century.[7] But the underlying drama of sibling hostilities goes back even further: to the primal story of Cain and Abel, recorded in Hebrew Scripture; or the myth of Herse and Aglauros, found in Ovid's *Metamorphoses*.

For many of us, the best known of the "Cinderella" variants come from continental Europe: Giambattista Basile (Italy, 1636), Charles Perrault (France, 1697, the most direct source for the Disney version of the 1960s), and the Grimm brothers (Germany, 1812). While details vary, the central conflict remains the same: one innocent sibling is maltreated by her elders (and by her stepmother), until her natural beauty and virtue result in her status elevation—even as her competitors' ugliness and malice lead to their downfall.

Bruno Bettelheim traces the developmental conflict of the Cinderella story to the end of the Oedipal phase—a time after children have lived through the intensity of rivalry with their parents (treated in stories like "Snow White"). Troubled by the recognition of their own murderous fantasies, subjected to increasing criticism as the demands of socialization are more strictly enforced (by toilet training, for example), post-Oedipal children begin to question their place in the world's affections. An older sibling may seem unbearably more accomplished; a younger sibling may get far too much attention. Thus, the child takes comfort in identifying with Cinderella, the underappreciated sibling who is maltreated by others yet ends up living happily ever after. At the same time, the child discovers she would rather not be identified with the ugly stepsisters—and so, learns by bad example the value of tempering impulses to envy.

One detail of the Cinderella story dear to Freudian analysts is the lost shoe, whose perfect fit identifies the true heroine in the end. The slipper made of glass is Perrault's innovation for the French court as well as the image Disney chose to ensconce in the American cultural imagination. Some scholars of folklore have speculated, though, that the "glass slipper" was actually a mistake: since the French words *vair* (fur) and *verre* (glass) sound alike, these authorities assume that Perrault misheard a folk tale about a fur bootie and turned it, improbably, into a shoe made of glass. Bettelheim, however, disputes this theory. After all, he insists, for the shoe test to make sense as a means of identifying the young woman who fled from the court, the slipper must be made of some material that will not stretch to fit any but its rightful owner. From this point, it is but a small step to his conclusion:

> A tiny receptacle into which some part of the body can slip and fit tightly can be seen as a symbol of the vagina. Something that is brittle and must not be stretched because it would break reminds us of the hymen; and something that is easily lost at the end of a ball . . . seems an appropriate image for virginity.[8]

Thus, when the prince slides the shoe onto Cinderella's outstretched foot at the climax of the story—just as when the groom slides a ring onto a bride's outstretched finger—he is symbolically "deflowering" her, demonstrating how perfectly their bodies will fit together in a life of marital bliss.

Cinderella's Siblings: A Jungian View

Freudian analysts are not the only ones to find that fairy tales are rich with insights into the psychological crises of growing up. Ann and Barry Ulanov, for example, interpret the Cinderella story from a contrasting Jungian perspective.[9] From their vantage point, the conflict between Cinderella and her stepsisters is not simply an example of rivalry between siblings. It also represents a conflict between the ego and "shadow" within each of us.

In Jungian terminology, the shadow consists of aspects of our personalities that our egos would like to disown because they interfere with the more flattering self-image we prefer. Clearly, envy lives within the shadow's world. We dislike acknowledging that we begrudge the successes of others—whether of our siblings or other perceived rivals. Instead, we project these uncomfortable feelings outside of ourselves. In dreams and fairy tales, we personify such shadow contents as entirely unattractive figures—trolls, giants, wicked witches, vindictive stepmothers, and nasty stepsisters.

For Jungian analysts, psychological integration demands that we recognize the shadow's contents as part of ourselves. Only then can we learn what they have to teach us. In the case of envy, this means discovering our own "voracious hunger for the good"—a hunger we initially experience as emptiness and frustration because its intensity seems insatiable. We feel as if we will *never* have our hearts' desire, and so we grow angry at those who are enjoying successes that elude us. Since we cannot understand why *they* should be so happy and *we*, so miserable, we develop an explanation to cope with our confusion: the envied persons must be to blame for our misfortune. They must be intentionally thwarting and depriving us. Cinderella has stolen "our" prince; Abel has stolen "our" place in God's affections; Amber Heath has stolen "our daughter's" spot on the cheerleading squad. Only when we stop denying our envy or projecting it outward can we come to grips with the deep longings that drive us. Only then can we integrate the energies of the shadow into our fuller selfhood and pursue in more constructive ways the good for which we yearn.

In other words, we are not just the spiteful stepsiblings of fairy tale fame. If we do the hard work of "individuation"—the Jungian term for growing into our full and distinctive selfhood—we, too, can become Cinderella: "fit" to stand in our own shoes and not hanker after those of others; "wedded" with the cross-gendered aspects of our personalities (*anima* or *animus*, for a Jungian) that make us complete. For, not only do all of us have a shadow side represented by the ugly stepsisters of the story, we also have an impulse toward the wholeness we find embodied in the tale's heroic figure. Cinderella on her hearth is a Vestal Virgin, servant of a sacred flame, burned by the fires of envy—whether shooting from the hateful gaze of other people, or smoldering in hidden parts of her own psyche—yet rising reborn from the ashes at the end of the story.

Envy and Gratitude: Melanie Klein

Less well-known than either the Freudian or Jungian perspectives on envy, but at least as significant, is the work of Melanie Klein. Like Bettelheim, Klein is a neo-Freudian who takes her predecessor's categories of childhood psychosexual development in distinctive directions. Unlike Bettelheim, she focuses neither on the Oedipal nor the sibling-rivalry roots of our envious feelings. Rather, her analytic gaze extends even further back: to the baby at the mother's breast.

For Klein, the baby experiences its most intense moments of enjoyment and gratification at the feeding breast (or its surrogate, the bottle).

However, such moments are rarely as perfect as the child, newly separated from the ceaseless nurture of life in the womb, would wish. Inevitably, even with the most devoted parenting, frustrations arise: the milk comes too quickly or too slowly; the parent holds too tightly or not tightly enough; the person doing the feeding is in a hurry or anxious or depressed; the child craves the breast at a time when it is not available to suckle. At such moments, the baby experiences distress and confusion. Because he is far too young to understand what is happening, Klein writes, "he feels that the gratification of which he was deprived has been kept for itself by the breast that frustrated him."[10] In response, the baby grows envious of "the mean and grudging breast," wanting to "spoil" and destroy it as the source of his misery.

Of course, none of this occurs at the level of conscious thought. Rather, it occurs at a depth of feeling that opens up in the infant a reservoir for experiences of envy later in life. Thus, any time in the future when we encounter a person who has power over us, particularly the power to give or withhold something that we crave (affection, praise, fulfillment of whatever kind), we dip into our reservoir of infantile "breast envy." Our admiration of the other person's attractiveness and potency grows soured by the impotence we feel in comparison.

Both Klein and the Ulanovs apply this insight to ways in which envy interferes with therapeutic relationships. One of the goals of therapy is for the counselor to become, through transference, the good parent who is the trustworthy source of unconditional care. But this also puts the therapist in the position of becoming, in Kleinian terms, the "satisfactory breast"—the object that is not only loved for the gratification it gives but also hated for the abundance it seems to enjoy relative to the recipient's own neediness. Under such circumstances, to accept any insight from the therapist can feel like adding more feathers to an already well-feathered cap, while the client slumps, hat in hand, disproportionately dependent all over again. Thus, patients may resist getting well out of spite, resenting any credit they think their analysts might get for their recovery. Or they may criticize and argue against any offered help, biting the metaphoric hand (or breast) that offers food, ultimately damaging themselves more than anyone else.

A related set of insights shows Klein's helpfulness for thinking concretely about envy in our own lives. She catalogs a number of defense mechanisms we enact to protect ourselves from the most acute pangs of such poisonous feelings. Closest to the preceding discussion is the *refusal of help*: the "No, thank you, I can take care of this all by myself" when in fact none of us can effectively survive without assistance from others. A second defense is *idealization*. Rather than view the people we envy—whether therapists or teachers, coworkers or neighbors—as possessing both advantages and flaws, we exercise selective vision, seeing only the "charmed" aspects of their lives; in so doing, we explain to ourselves how we could not possibly be expected to compete with such paragons. A third defense is *indifference* and *withdrawal*. If we repeatedly find it too painful to compete and lose, we finally decide not to enter the fray at all.

Withdrawal and indifference can quickly turn, however, from apathetic to angry, radiating in waves of hostility. *Devaluation of self*, a fourth defense against envy, often marches in tandem with idealization. Aiming the lens of selective perception at myself, I see my life as exclusively cursed where my rival is uniquely charmed. I am fat and ugly, and she is gorgeous; I am stupid and sluggish, and she is brilliant; I will never succeed at anything, so I might as well not try (here we see withdrawal again), whereas she will effortlessly walk away with all available prizes. Concluding that life is not fair, I may then project anger onto my rival. In a fifth form of defense, I lash out, if not physically, then verbally, *disparaging the other* with cattiness and slander. Think again of the prominent place given to detraction and grumbling as offshoots of envy in the cardinal sins tradition. A final defense mechanism identified by Klein is the hostile attempt *to stir up envy in others* through bragging about our own achievements and possessions. Clearly, this is the one-upping tendency at which so much contemporary advertising is aimed—the eat-your-heart-out satisfaction derived from outdoing the mythical Joneses by the cars we drive, the cell phones we use, or even the perfume we wear.

"Not Good Enough": Harold Boris

Melanie Klein hypothesizes that a certain amount of envy comes with the territory of being human. No sooner are we born than we reach for the breast or bottle; when it is not there exactly when we want it, we respond with frustration and rage. Temperamental differences will lead us to experience this disappointment in varying ways: for some children, it will be mild and short-lived; for others, acute and pervasive. Further factors play into the equation: differing physiological thresholds of discomfort, for example, or different patterns of parental care. Thus, while envy may be developmentally inevitable, modes of expressing it will vary widely.

Harold Boris accounts for this variance by positing that envy is born of a childhood experience of feeling *not good enough*: not merely unwanted, but "unselected."[11] Some infants, he suggests, feel a dread that they do not deserve to live at all, much less to thrive. Yet, they see around themselves others who flourish. To the eye of the anxiety-ridden child (or adult), such lucky others apparently do not experience the same qualms about their "good-enough-ness" or "fitness" for life. Thus, these others become targets for rage, resentment, and envy.

In Boris's opinion, some of the difference between feeling selected or unselected roots in patterns of nurture: the child who is not "fed" responsively—whether with milk or with attention—may have extraordinary difficulty in learning to deal with issues of longing and frustration throughout life. But for some people, even highly attentive parental care does not protect against the inclination to envy. Boris offers a bold, if troubling, Darwinian explanation. In the struggle for survival, he says, some have what it takes to win, and others—the "runts of the litter"—do not. Envy is the emotional response of those "runts" to the inevitability that they will lose.

There is likely a germ of truth to this theory. If we think about people we know, we probably recognize some who seem to walk around with chronic grudges, convinced that they have received or will receive the short end of any stick, ready to interpret even unintended slights as major offenses. For whatever reason, some people grow up with a "low hate / high love threshold," to borrow the helpful phrase of psychologist Joseph Berke.[12] Children with a low hate threshold, Berke writes, "hoard hurts like squirrels garner nuts." Some among us may be genetically predisposed to hoard hurts, seeing the world as unfair and thus be ever ready to favor resentment over reconciliation when provoked.

Still, two crucial cautions are in order. First, we need to be careful not to draw any quick conclusions about what traits assure a human's fitness for survival. Boris's language about the unselected or the runts of the litter could lead to dangerous conclusions that certain *types* of people (of certain races, genders, sexual orientations, or levels of ability) are doomed to be less wanted than others and therefore more envious *by nature*. The second caution follows. Even if an individual or group is predisposed to envy, this does not provide an excuse to stop working to control or minimize the damage done by such a disposition. After all, poor ability to handle alcohol may be genetically linked, but this does not excuse the abusive behaviors connected with alcoholism. Likewise, with envy: Even if invidious passions should happen to be a natural part of the human condition, driven by biological urges to survive and thrive, moralists may still have significant things to say about their appropriate tempering and control.

Turf Love

These cautions pose a provocative question for further exploration. How natural—that is to say, how inevitable a part of our genetic makeup—is envy? To respond moves us from Harold Boris's speculative hypotheses to the more sustained analyses of evolutionary psychology. Evolutionary psychologists work to trace human behavior to its genetic underpinnings. Of each behavior, trait, or attitude explored, they ask: How does this practice enhance the organism's potential to survive—particularly, to reproduce and pass along its genetic material to the next generation? They assume that practices enhancing our capacity to pass along our genetic material to future generations—our reproductive fitness—will be *selected* by the evolutionary process, whereas practices failing to promote such genetic survival will eventually disappear.

What behaviors enhance reproductive fitness in human beings? The answer involves both competitive and cooperative form of conduct. We compete for the most turf, the most status, the most promising mates; yet we also cooperate in activities like food-gathering and community protection. If we do not compete, we cannot assure ourselves of the strongest genetic re-combinations possible. But if we do not cooperate, we do not stand a chance of nurturing those re-combinations (otherwise known as our biological children) into maturity, at which point they themselves can pass our chromosomal code on to a further generation.

How does an emotion like envy fit into this picture? The fact that we continue to experience envy through generation after generation of human existence means that something about the experience must contribute to survival value, or so evolutionary psychologists claim. Otherwise, it would simply have withered away, like gills or a vestigial tail. So, what valuable contributions does envy offer? The short answer is that feelings of envy motivate us to pursue a competitive advantage over our rivals, while cooperating with those we perceive to be underdogs like ourselves.

Terence Kealey, a lecturer in clinical biochemistry at Cambridge, goes so far as to suggest that "envy is inevitable because it is good for our genes."[13] The more wives or concubines a man has, the stronger are his chances of passing his genetic code into the next generation. Instead of being content with one or two partners, he will thus be prompted by envy of a neighbor's four or five to pursue even more. In like manner, the more conspicuous goods a male parades, whether in appearance or possessions or accomplishments, the likelier he is to be viewed as a desirable partner by females on the lookout for someone to provide a strong genetic endowment and future security for their offspring. Thus, envy prompts women to seek after—and, ultimately, sleep with—the possessor(s) of those endowments that might otherwise give the genetic bonus to their neighbors' rather than their own children.

However we may feel about the gender stereotypes in such examples, we can see their fundamental point. Genetic wiring for contentment would not promote the drive toward reproductive advantage nearly as effectively as genetic wiring for discontent. Evolutionary psychologists further suggest that this discontent is triggered by comparison with those closest to us. What matters is not that we acquire some absolute number of desirable possessions or partners or progeny, but simply that we acquire *more* than our immediate rivals. Such a comparative perspective ultimately enables us to conserve energy: we know both when we need to compete and when we have attained enough that we can stop competing and turn to other tasks demanding our attention.[14]

Award-winning science writer Robert Wright gives a fuller explanation of the link between envy and the biologically desirable pursuit of competitive advantage. Wright suggests that what evolution selects is not envy itself but the "emotional equipment" or "mental organs" that produce the experience of envy. Envy itself may, in fact, be an unfortunate by-product of those organs (as flatulence may be an unfortunate by-product of the way fiber gets digested in our intestines); yet the organs and processes themselves are too valuable for us to do without.[15] The organs and processes that give rise to envy play key roles in our struggle for reproductive advantage. These roles are bound up in the evolutionary survival of hierarchies that characterize social groups, from the pecking order of chickens to the pack order of wolves. Such hierarchies appear with particular complexity in primate societies—among gorillas, chimps, bonobos, or human beings. From the orchestration of ritual greetings (who assumes submissive postures relative to whom), to the allocation of goods such as "turf" or food or desirable mates, the organization of life in primate groupings demonstrates the existence of a status ladder. The highest rungs of this ladder are occupied by dominant individuals who have won the most fights—or successfully established among their peers that they *would* win, if anyone were foolish enough to challenge their supremacy.

Wright concludes that once such a status ladder exists and occupying a higher rung will produce a reproductive payoff, genes that assist us in climbing the ladder without excessive cost will be selected. These genes may work by positive or negative reinforcement. Positively, such genes and the mental organs they produce instill drives like ambition and pleasurable emotions like pride when we succeed in achieving our goals. By extension, invidious passions in their benign forms of admiration and the desire to emulate the achievements of others work to our genetic advantage by positively reinforcing our motivation to strive for improvement.

On the other hand, the genes responsible for envy may work in tandem with less pleasant emotional experiences, provoking feelings of shame when we fail to realize our ambitions. Invidious passions in their malign forms of sadness or hostility over a rival's success—what we called in chapter 2 "envy proper"—supply negative feedback, prompting us to take measures to avoid such feelings in the future. They may, for example, stimulate us to band together with others we view as underdogs like ourselves, cooperating to our mutual advantage against the more powerful members of our cohort. Wright even posits that *gossip*—one of Capital Envy's offspring and one of the ways underdogs traditionally soothe their one-down feelings—has social uses insofar as it spreads the kind of information that supports reproductive fitness: who is sleeping with whom; who is meeting with extraordinary fortune or failure. From this perspective, a certain amount of discomfort with lower status serves a positive evolutionary function. Even an excruciating amount of such discomfort may have its uses, protecting us from expending energy on contests we could only lose.

Ill-Fitting Genes

However, even if we conclude with the evolutionary psychologists that there is survival value in our love for "turf" and our desire to have more of it than our rivals, we still remain a far cry from demonstrating that envy proper is good for us as a species or as individuals. The fact that our genes make us do or feel any particular thing does not thereby justify it—however much our de-moralized, triumphantly commercial culture might wish us to believe otherwise. Thus, I cannot agree with Kealey, who ends his exploration of the genetic basis of envy by observing: "sociological Darwinism offers a better explanation for the development of the evolutionarily useful, so-called deadly sin, envy, than do religion or the traditional humanities. We scientists are entitled to a little pride."[16]

While he is right that evolutionary psychology enhances our understanding of the biological impulses that root envious passions so deeply in our psyches, he seems a bit quick to minimize the so-called sinful aspects of such experiences and to discount the further insights of religion and the humanities into their potential causes and cures.

After all, as human animals, we are products of our culture as well as of our nature, and our cultures have good reasons for educating us in how to restrain impulses that are otherwise embedded in us by generations of evolutionary history. Darwin himself was keen on this fact, noting that human beings instruct one another in moral behavior, using complex language systems to pass along codes of conduct that contribute to the common good. Consequently, an appreciation for the evolutionary roots of any given behavior need not lead us to its uncritical endorsement; some genes may not "fit" us very well for life with one another and may require cultural alterations.

Religion and the humanities work to promote cultural alterations for the sake of the common good of which Darwin speaks. In fact, these disciplines advance our understanding of envy in three key ways. They assist us with precise definitions of terms, with comparative cultural analysis and with differentiation of "moral" from "natural" activity—or, as ethicists put it, of "ought" from merely "is."

Precise definition of terms is the issue that preoccupied us for much of our second chapter. Much depends on what we mean when we talk about envy—whether we argue that it is a natural, inevitable, and even advantageous part of our evolutionary makeup to be tolerated and perhaps even celebrated; or whether we argue that it is a deadly sin to be disciplined and eradicated insofar as possible. Simply to equate envy with competitive drive and desire to excel—with "turf love"—seems a bit hasty. There is a world of difference between my wanting to have as many bananas (or whatever) as my next-door neighbors and my wanting to spoil their food supply simply to keep them from having it, when doing so will not improve the resources available to me or my family. There is a world of difference between wanting to become the leader of the pack and being so eaten up with resentment when my leadership skills are not recognized that I retreat into embittered scheming. Even if we grant that hostile envious feelings may foster temporary alliances of underdogs among whom snarling and backbiting serve to reinforce opposition to the more powerful members of a group, we also need to notice that such alliances are less stable than ones formed around positive goals. After all, anyone who delights in sharing malicious conversation with me about a third party is just as likely under different circumstances to delight in spreading malice about me to others.

In short, if we fail to work out definitions that distinguish between "striving" and "spitefulness" or "emulation" and "envy proper," we run the risk of mistaking dynamics that undermine individual and corporate fitness with ones that enhance it. Philosopher Jerome Neu summarizes the matter.[17] He points out that some schools of psychology claim we should try not to minimize envy but to optimize it, insofar as "a certain amount of envy is developmentally necessary." But, he insists, we need to distinguish carefully between "*admiring* envy (which may be necessary for an ego ideal, and so beneficial) and *malicious* envy (which the world could just as well do without)." The desire to raise the self (as we saw in chapter 2) differs significantly from the desire to lower the other. "Do these disparate desires really have a common instinctual source?" Neu asks. "Is it really inconceivable that we might overcome the sources of malicious envy without doing damage to the necessary foundations of the ego ideal"—or, for that matter, the necessary foundations of evolutionary fitness?

Comparative analysis suggests that different human groups throughout the world have in fact found ways of overcoming, or at least minimizing, the sources of malicious envy. Anthropologists have studied a variety of cultures to see how they deal with issues of rivalry and competition. If the evolutionary psychologists are right, we should expect to see universal evidence of the "genes" (Kealey) or "mental organs" (Wright) for envy at work: something that is part of human nature will, by definition, be present wherever human beings are found. Still, we may have to conclude that the genes or organs for an emotion-complex like envy are more like the genes or organs for a human-animal process like language than those for a nonhuman-animal process like digestion. Digestion, after all, works basically the same way whether it is working on french fries, fava beans, or falafel. Language, on the other hand, produces sounds and structures as distinctive as Swedish and Swahili, depending upon the cultural context that shapes it.

In his book *No Contest*, writer Alfie Kohn shares our concern with those who "play the 'human nature' card" in an effort to argue that rivalry is an innate and inevitable product of natural selection.[18] He points out that Darwin's so-called "struggle for existence" really involves significant measures of cooperation both within and among species, and "survival of the fittest" has to do simply with passing our genetic material along to the next generation—not with quashing our opponents for a place on the cheerleading squad or provoking the Joneses to eat their hearts out because we have acquired a car or smart phone more sophisticated than theirs. Admittedly, somewhere deep in our evolutionary brains we may correlate that cheerleading spot or cell phone with the prospect of attaining a desirable mate with whom to transmit our genetic code into the future. But by this point in our history, the cultural overlay between the species-wide survival impulse and its embodiment in our individual lives has grown pretty thick. Just as we learn different languages using the mental organs that evolution has shaped for that purpose, we also learn different complexes of meanings to attach to possessions, achievements, and accolades. Is it that far-fetched to imagine a culture for which the most "attractive" mates are self-sacrificing exemplars of generosity and gratitude, rather than self-promoting possessors of the most "toys"?

This question resonates with the one posed by Jerome Neu: is it really inevitable for human beings to indulge in malicious comparisons with one another, eager to succeed even at the cost of others' misfortune? By way of response, Kohn's research answers: No, it is not inevitable at all. Culture after culture shows us that there is nothing natural about the American way of competition. Comparative studies between Anglo-American and Mexican children reveal that the former are far more inclined than the latter to take a playmate's toy away simply for spite, even when they have ample toys of their own and have no intention of playing with the pilfered object. Anglo-American children cannot stop competing, even in games arranged to reward cooperative behavior, whereas Mexican children enter into cooperative strategies with far greater ease. In experimental games, Norwegians demonstrate two times more likelihood than Americans for responding to cooperation with cooperation. Blackfoot Indian children, Israeli kibbutzniks, Australian aborigines, the Inuit of Canada, the Tangu of Papua New Guinea all display marked preferences for games in which the goal is teamwork and the achievement of a tie, rather than games where a single victor makes off with all the spoils. In a very telling sentence for our purposes, Kohn even notes that the Mixtecans of Juxtlahuaca, Mexico, "regard envy and competitiveness as a minor crime."[19]

In light of such comparisons, we might wonder which of these cultures are actually the more advanced and which are the more primitive. Granted, our "de-moralized society" could easily wipe off the map a social grouping whose members criminalize envy and other rivalrous behaviors. We would even have a choice of weapons at our disposal: military, economic, or the more subtle imperialisms of culture. But does this preeminence of power truly mean that we are more "fit" than these other cultures to survive? Or do we not instead see creeping signs of "unfitness" all around us in the United States of the early third millennium: on the social front, vandalism, theft, larceny, murder or attempted murder, increasing unrest between haves and have-nots, and patterns of consumption that wreak havoc on our natural environment; on the personal front, ulcers, heart disease, addictions, the physical and mental toll of striving to get ahead and stay ahead, or feeling miserable if we cannot? Under such circumstances, would retraining ourselves and our children to view envy as a "crime"—or, borrowing from our own heritage, a "deadly sin"—be so counterproductive?

At this juncture, the religionists and moralists among us begin to step onto our own home turf. Having defined our terms more precisely, having examined cross-cultural analyses, we have a third angle to explore in assessing the fitness of any so-called "genes" for envy: a differentiation between is and ought, a distinction between the ways we instinctively feel inclined to act and the ways we morally direct our activity in pursuit of a common good. Over a century ago, in the debate concerning evolutionary ethics that raged during the heyday of Social Darwinism, philosopher Thomas Henry Huxley posed the is/ought dilemma well. Is it the ultimate aim of our cultures, he asked, to promote "the survival of the fittest . . . [or rather] the fitting of as many as possible to survive?" [20]

As a theologian and ethicist, I am inclined to give preference to the latter goal. Interestingly enough, so is Robert Wright. "That natural selection has opted for social inequality in our species," he concludes, "certainly doesn't make inequality *right*; and it makes it inevitable in only a limited sense." Thus, within our immediate social groupings, we do create hierarchies; someone will more likely than not emerge as the more powerful member of any given group, the one whose opinions are deferred to, the one whose approval is sought. "But," Wright asserts, "social inequality in the larger sense—gross disparities in wealth and privilege across a whole nation—is another matter. That is a product of government policy or lack of policy."[21] To such larger matters of social policy we now turn.

Chapter Six

Polis Envy

In 1831, a twenty-five-year-old French aristocrat set out on a journey to learn about democracy.[1] The idea of government by the people-at-large rather than by a hereditary ruling class was still novel and, in many circles, suspect. In France, it was tarred with the bloody excesses of the French Revolution, which had rapidly deteriorated from a democratic revolt to a dictatorship, only gradually returning to a monarchy with uneasy constitutional compromises. Many of the young man's relatives had been put to death by the guillotine during the Reign of Terror. His parents, imprisoned while barely in their twenties, were saved from execution only by the toppling of Robespierre three days before their sentence was to be carried out.

Historians say that Alexis de Tocqueville's mother never fully recovered from the trauma. His father, the Count de Tocqueville, recovered sufficiently to accept a position in the government of the restored monarch, Charles X. When Alexis completed his law degree at age twenty-two, the count secured a government appointment for him as well. But Charles X, high-handed in dissolving a legislature that disagreed with his kingly prerogatives, was ousted by an uprising in 1830. The senior Tocqueville withdrew from government. The junior took an oath of loyalty to the new, more liberal government under King Louis-Philippe I but recognized that his position as the member of an aristocratic family left him in some danger.

To stay out of political turmoil at home, Alexis de Tocqueville decided to travel abroad. To signal his loyalty to the new regime, he cast his travels as a government business: a trip to the still-youthful United States of America to study the prison system. However, he had far more than prisons in view. He was fascinated by the whole democratic experiment, curious to see how a government would take shape in a country with no hereditary aristocracy and what kind of character would emerge in people who forged their own destiny rather than having it assigned to them by birth. Gifted with listening skills to match his restless intellect, he conducted extensive interviews throughout his travel. After returning to France, he published the observations drawn from these interviews in a book titled *Democracy in America*, a work still hailed for its extraordinary insights.

Tocqueville made a few pointed observations about the relationship between democracy and envy. A half century before him, Benjamin Franklin had suggested that citizens of the newly formed United States would be free from envy insofar as hard work rather than accidents of birth would dictate their fortunes; hence, they would be able to apply their energies to achieving what they wanted rather than pining for privileges that could never be theirs.[2] Tocqueville was less optimistic. As both historical and modern-day analysts agree, the experience of envy tends to be fueled by twin engines of proximity and possibility. We are more inclined to envy someone who is relatively close to us in status; evolutionary psychology, as we just saw, posits this focus on outdoing our nearest rivals as a mechanism for conserving energy, showing us when we can stop competing for resources and focus attention on other survival tasks instead. Further, we are more inclined to feel envy in situations when we might actually have had a shot at rewards that have gone elsewhere. The theme song of envy is "I could have been a contender," not "It wasn't in the stars for me to win." The former is resentful; the latter, merely resigned. Insofar as democratic societies foster greater social proximity and individual possibility, they may actually *invite* rather than eliminate envy. Tocqueville noted this risk, declaring: "Democratic institutions awaken and foster a passion for equality which they can never entirely satisfy."[3] In a self-professed "land of opportunity," we talk as if everyone *ought* to be able to excel. But not everyone will. What then? Unfortunately, the seeds of ambition we have sowed—with lofty rhetoric and good intentions—will be ripe to grow into weeds of disappointment and discontent.

Tocqueville's analysis has proved insightful in yet another way. Given what he assumed to be a basic human tendency to seek after marks of distinction (to climb the "status ladder," as the evolutionary psychologists of chapter 5 would have put it), he noted that in contexts where rank was not clearly given, we would be forced to invent it. What would be the medium of our invention? Not dress code or title or any of the other traditional accompaniments of class rank with which he was acquainted from his years in France, but *money*. Consequently, he cautioned: "Among democratic nations, ambition is ardent and continual, but its aim is not habitually lofty; and life is generally spent in eagerly coveting small objects."[4] But to be precise, we do not crave the objects in themselves so much as the status attached to them. Lacking the security of social positions defined for us by birth, we must check constantly to see how our neighbors are doing—most visibly, what they own—to verify that we measure up.

Envy Management

Such status comparisons are a mixed blessing. They can fuel competition in ways that foster an inventive spirit and stimulate a growth economy (as we saw with the triumph of the commercial in chapter 1). But they can also turn neighbors into rivals more concerned with besting one another than with bettering their broader communities.

Given such destructive potential, societies throughout history have developed strategies of envy management. The democracy of ancient Athens, for example, practiced the curious custom of ostracism. At an annual assembly, citizens could nominate for expulsion from the state any person who was deemed a threat to public morale. Votes were cast by writing the offending person's name on a shard of pottery (an *ostrakon*: hence "ostracism"). The historian Plutarch explained that this practice was not a punishment for wickedness but rather a means by which a community could lessen envy by temporarily removing from its midst any members whose "preeminence" put them "out of step with democratic equality."[5]

Other practices of envy management seem less severe. Rituals of gift-giving, for example: in many cultures, the "haves" extend largesse to the "have nots," thereby deflecting—or, less charitably, buying off—potential envy. Think of the tradition of Boxing Day in the United Kingdom, celebrated on the day after Christmas as an occasion for employers to give gifts to servants and tradespeople. Think, in the United States, of the custom of providing favors to all the children who attend a birthday party or giving gifts to the bridesmaids and groomsmen at a wedding. Among some Native American peoples of the northwest coast, the ceremony of the potlatch offered wealthy individuals an opportunity to demonstrate their status by how much they gave away to guests at the lavish feasts they hosted. In a related fashion, many primal communities practiced rituals of sharing, cooperating to assure that products from the hunt or other bounty would be distributed within the group. Such practices survived in this country in the frontier etiquette of barn raising and continue to be in evidence when natural disasters, like Hurricanes Katrina or Sandy, prompt an outpouring of support from those who "but for the grace of God" might find themselves in similar straits.

Philosophical and theological worldviews can also serve an envy-management role. In aristocratic societies predating the transitional era in which Alexis de Tocqueville lived, belief that God had ordained a strict social hierarchy kept people from aspiring above their appointed stations. Some might even suggest that the church's labeling of envy as a deadly sin served a conservative political function, discouraging people in lower social positions from rising up in protest. Yet, prohibitions against envy can also be seen as a motor rather than a brake to social progress. Where envy is frowned upon, the excellent are given permission to excel without fear of negative consequences (such as literal ostracism). Meanwhile, those less gifted—whether by God, native endowment, or lucky circumstances—are discouraged from "eating their hearts out" in discontent and encouraged instead to pursue the successes of which they *are* capable.

The Politics of Envy?

One cultural practice of potential envy management requires separate treatment, given its controversial place in contemporary debates: that of redistributing wealth through taxation and social welfare programs. It seems clear that such redistribution can play a role in tempering envy, leveling the playing field of opportunity and helping to fulfill the passion for equality that Tocqueville saw as an outgrowth of democracy. What is less clear, however, is whether such calls for redistribution are prompted by envy. Teachers may work hard to avoid favoritism and treat all their students fairly. Such efforts surely help to keep some forms of envy at bay, but would we identify them as motivated by a "pedagogy of envy"?

When the teacher in question is the so-called "nanny state," some commentators do name envy as the operating motive. In the 1990s, Doug Bandow, a Christian libertarian, coined the phrase "politics of envy" to describe then-current social policies. His initial target was the so-called "soak the rich" tax plan of the Clinton administration. For Bandow, progressive rather than flat-rate taxation stems from a desire "to loot wealthier classes." "People," he says, "don't so much want more money for themselves as they want to take it away from those with more."[6]

He is not alone in such arguments; entering the phrase "politics of envy" in an Internet search engine generates hundreds of commentators who have jumped on the Bandow wagon. Charges that originated in the Clinton era continue to surface decades later. The *Los Angeles Times* (January 10, 2012) reported on a speech Mitt Romney gave after his victory in the New Hampshire primary, in which he responded to President Obama's references to a growing chasm between the 99 percent and the 1 percent of wealth holders in the United States, saying: "This country . . . has a leader who divides us with the bitter politics of envy." Questioned by Matt Lauer the next morning on *The Today Show* as to whether such a label was in fact appropriate to sum up all concerns about the regulation of financial institutions or the distribution of wealth in this country, Romney reiterated his claim: "It's about envy. It's about class warfare."[7]

But is it really? Interestingly enough, such accusations constitute the one form of contemporary discourse in which the term "envy" still carries moral weight, contrasting sharply with the cavalier, envy-provoking attitude of the triumphantly commercial ("eat your heart out") or the comforting, envy-assuaging attitude of the triumphantly therapeutic ("Don't be ashamed: it's only natural"). So, we have particularly good reason to examine how appropriately the label is being used.

A first step in our examination leads us to recall envy's connection to proximity and possibility. As defined in chapter 2, envy is "the pained perception of an unfavorable difference in status between the self and a rival on a scale of personally significant values." How likely is someone earning $25,000 a year to view someone making $2.5 million as an economic "rival"? Clinical psychologist Josh Gressel concludes in a recent book on envy, "We [of moderate incomes] are less likely to envy the wealth of the super-rich because its stratospheric quality is not seen as a basis for self-evaluation."[8] We may feel gnawing pangs when our coworker gets a bigger salary bump than we do. But the possibility that our buying power would ever match that of Bill Gates or Warren Buffett seems too remote to generate significant personal distress.

Still, one could argue that the communications explosion of the late-twentieth century has made it possible for more people than ever to get a close-up look at "lifestyles of the rich and famous," thereby creating at least an illusion of proximity. Further, an illusion of possibility may be fueled by the phenomenal salaries that young people see being paid to athletes and performers not much older than they, or the enormous payouts offered by the lottery. So, perhaps the contexts of social comparison are changing. Those who warn about a "politics of envy" are at least right in showing us where as a culture we need to be on our guard.

A second consideration about the aptness of the "politics of envy" label takes us back to our analysis of the grammar of envy proper in chapter 2. There, we noted that it does not make grammatical or conceptual sense to say that I am envious *on behalf of* some other person or group; envy always takes the self as its subject. Yet, those who argue for reallocation of resources at the national level—raising taxes on the uppermost one percent so as to extend the safety net for the poorest of the poor—are generally not proposing a plan from which they *personally* stand to benefit. Rather, they are seeking benefits on behalf of a third party: people less economically and politically advantaged than they.

Still, an advocate of the "politics of envy" charge might remind us of a further aspect of the definition of envy proper, which is not only a "pained perception of an unfavorable difference in status between the self and a rival," but also a desire to correct that imbalance "by raising the self or lowering the other." As we noted in chapter 2, envy in its most malicious forms can be satisfied simply by seeing the other taken down a peg, even if the envious person gets no other direct benefit. So, Bandow insinuated, the proponents of "soak the rich" taxation are not really interested in using that money to benefit themselves or anyone else; they just want the rich not to have it. If his charge is right, then the diagnosis of envy is more appropriate. The question remaining becomes a factual and not a moral one: Are the advocates of redistributed wealth proposing to do anything beneficial with the redistribution?

This question leads us to the third and most significant consideration in assessing the "politics of envy" label. Envy touches us at a deeply, and sometimes embarrassingly, intimate level. For this reason, we are likely to keep envy proper to ourselves; even after the efforts of commercial and therapeutic culture to remove its moral sting, we are still loath to admit to feelings of inferiority from having been outdone by our close competitors. But other emotions that resemble envy are less attuned to *personal* slight than to violations of *principle* and are thus more likely to be given a public airing. Two related emotions that come under this other heading are *resentment* and *indignation*. We are resentful when we think an injustice has been done—principally to ourselves but also to some person or group with which we identify. As taxpayers, whether on the right or the left of the political spectrum, we *resented* the fact that *our* tax dollars were used to bail out financial institutions in 2008, which then turned around in 2009 and paid bonuses totaling in the hundreds of millions to executives who had been in power when the firms initially went under.

Resentment tends to focus inward, fuming over the unfairness it perceives. Indignation, on the other hand, focuses outward. This is the emotion captured by the Aristotelian term *nemesis*, linked to a verb meaning "distribute" and to the goddess of distributive justice. Nemesis or indignation is involved when we perceive that justice has been violated, either because another's success is ill-gotten or because our own lack of success results from unfairness. However, instead of fixating (as with resentment) on the injury, we devote our energies to protest and our efforts to improve the situation. However we feel about its strategies, the Occupy Wall Street movement might be seen as an enactment of indignation.

Of course, as we also noted in chapter 2, it is all too easy to rationalize our motives to ourselves as we slip down the slope from righteous indignation to self-righteous vindictiveness. In fragile and fallen human beings, envy and indignation can coexist and even feed one another. Thus, before we can clearly determine whether our era is plagued by a self-serving "politics of the envious" or by an equity-promoting "politics of the righteously indignant," we need to have a broader theory of justice in view.

A Theory of Justice

One of the most discussed theories of justice to be employed in the envy/equity debates is that crafted by John Rawls.[9] To enter into his theory, we need to undertake a thought experiment. Suppose we were given the opportunity to create the type of society in which we would ideally wish to live. We are not given the power to make money grow on trees: wealth will still have to be created through some type of production and exchange of goods. But we *are* given the power to invent the systems by which this production and exchange will operate: how factories, for example, will be managed; how workers and managers will be compensated; how goods will be priced and taxed; how revenue will be funneled back into the system, as wages for workers, profits for investors, funding for social programs, and the like.

There is just one catch to this exercise. We are conducting it behind what Rawls labels a "veil of ignorance." Behind this veil, we are unable to discover one crucial piece of information—namely, what role will we as individuals be allotted in the social order we are creating? Will we be workers or managers? Will we be born into a family whose wealth goes back multiple generations or to a family whose poverty goes back equally far?

One further pragmatic constraint on our thought experiment also applies: We do not have the freedom to create a Lake Wobegon, in which all the children—and all the adults—are "above average." People will still have diverse endowments. Some will be average or below average in certain areas; some will be smarter, or stronger, or more resourceful, or better looking. But again, we *do* have the opportunity to invent the systems by which such differences will be accommodated: scholarships, training programs, safety nets. The same catch as earlier, however, remains. From behind the veil of ignorance, we do not know what gifts and capacities *we* as individuals will be born with—or without.

In such a state of ignorance about how we are likely to be personally affected, Rawls says we will be motivated to create a system of maximum fairness. Thus, if I do not know whether I will be born with above average or below average intelligence, I will be inclined to shape a society in which those with fewer native gifts will have compensating opportunities for fulfillment: educational head-start programs, for example; jobs with fewer challenges but also fewer pressures. It is not required that in my efforts to create fairness, I also seek absolute equality. Certain people may still earn more money for doing jobs that require greater levels of education and training. The only requirement of fairness is that enough of their money be put to good use (in investment to create new jobs, incentives for risk-taking, philanthropy, taxation for social programs) that if roles were reversed and high earners came out from behind the veil of ignorance to find themselves reborn as low earners, they could still look at the system of rewards and find no cause for complaint. Rawls refers to this as the "difference principle": inequalities or "differences" of wealth or power are *just* if and only if they work to everyone's advantage, with the greatest benefit going to the least advantaged members of the society.

In elaborating this theory of justice, Rawls seems prophetically attuned to the "politics of envy" controversy of recent decades. He takes pains to distinguish between irrational, immoral envy and rational resentment (closer kin to what we have discussed above as indignation). He insists that, unlike envy, resentment is a "moral feeling" because it targets "unjust institutions or wrongful conduct" rather than personal desires and grudges.[10] The test to apply to any political proposal for allocating goods and services is whether we would use the same principles in cases where we ourselves did not stand to benefit—or, even better, to ones where we would potentially suffer a loss from their being followed. If so, then we are operating out of a theory of justice and not an attitude of envy or spite; we are appraising with ethically sensitive "veiled" eyes rather than morally suspect "green" ones.

The Ethics of Entitlement

Of course, not all theorists agree with Rawls. Robert Nozick, for example (another libertarian like Bandow), counters the Rawlsian definition of "justice as fairness" with something he calls "entitlement theory."[11] The choice of terms is potentially confusing. After all, government-administered "entitlement programs" (like welfare, unemployment compensation, or food stamps) redistribute wealth out of the very justice-as-fairness view that Nozick opposes. Further, in the years since Nozick published his theory, entitlement has come in popular speech to imply a spoiled or arrogant sense of privilege: the idea that life *owes* us something whether we have actually worked for it or not (the student who feels "entitled" to an A simply for showing up in class; the recent college graduate who feels "entitled" to a starting salary equivalent to that of someone who has worked for decades to achieve success). We will return to these other connotations in a moment, but we must first set them aside in order to understand Nozick's very different point. He would argue that, like Rawls, he is concerned with justice—in his case, justice for the *earner*. For Nozick, as long as a person has gained her wealth through just processes of acquisition and transfer, she is *entitled* to that wealth. To take it from her—for example, by redistributive taxation—is unjust (or, to use Rawls's own term, "unfair"). Thus, Nozick argues against any state intervention to equalize incomes.

Beyond this appeal to his own version of fairness (who better to decide how money should be used than the person who legitimately earned it in the first place?), Nozick's further argument is a pragmatic one. If our intent is to redistribute wealth as a way of preventing envy, then our efforts are destined to be fruitless. Human beings will always find *some* inequity to be unhappy about. If financial distinctions are eliminated, some other set of status differentiations will become important. Thus, rather than *restricting* the earnings of the wealthy, Nozick maintains that a society will be better served by *expanding* the number of dimensions along which people can gain self-esteem, such that income differences become less provocative of ill feelings. He makes a good point, helpfully countering a triumphantly commercial culture in which we are far too preoccupied with material measures of worth. But the proposal still seems oddly absolutist: just because a given measure will not completely eliminate a problem does not mean the measure is worthless. Nor is there any reason to suppose that we cannot do as Nozick suggests, expanding arenas for self-esteem while also providing access to the financial safety nets that are important to a baseline of well-being.

Nozick's next argument appeals to moral rather than practical considerations. Like the Bandow supporters who argue that a politics of envy is fomenting class warfare—or, for that matter, like the artists and moralists of the deadly sins tradition we have been exploring throughout this book—Nozick condemns envy as an immoral emotion. Precisely because this is so, he insists that we should not pander to it in the creation of public policy. After all, we do not typically restrict the advertising of high-calorie foods in order to protect the gluttonous from themselves. In Nozick's own example, we do not prohibit interracial couples from holding hands in public in order to keep racial bigots from becoming inflamed. Bigotry, like envy, is a wicked impulse. It is the problem of the person who *experiences* it, not of the one whose situation is seen as eliciting or provocative. Efforts to deal with the impulse—envious, bigoted, or gluttonous—should address the experience itself, not the external circumstances that occasion it. As moral theology has long maintained, there is a difference between an *offense given* and an *offense taken*. Nozick believes that to be bothered by income disparities is to *take* offense.

Again, however, we come to the question: Is all opposition to differences in income a matter of *envy*? Even if the super wealthy are not deliberately giving offense, flaunting their social position, should they remain exempt from any action by the state to redress acute imbalances? Both Nozick's points seem to take it as a given that programs to redistribute wealth are motivated by envy; but what if, instead, they are motivated by compassion for "the least of these"? Then, acting on them is not pandering to a wicked impulse but rather cultivating a noble one. Nozick is assuredly right that we will never eliminate envy no matter what social programs we enact. But by the same token, we will never eliminate disease, no matter how nutritious a diet we eat; is that a reason not to work against the food insecurity that means millions of children and senior citizens in our country go to bed hungry at night?

Unfortunately, disagreement seems inevitable between a view of justice insisting that individuals are "entitled" to keep all they have earned through their own efforts, and one equally insistent that some of these earnings should be redistributed through "entitlement programs" to individuals at the lowest ends of the economic spectrum, even if the lowest are where they are through no personal fault of the highest earners. Acting on a Rawlsian bias for the least advantaged carries with it the danger of overly protecting people from the consequences of their prior poor decisions or, worse, of encouraging "free riders," people who take advantage of government handouts while not lifting a hand to help themselves.

Whether we fall on Nozick's or Rawls's side of the political spectrum, we can agree that such "free riding" is shameful and deserves condemnation. But to lump all the disadvantaged into the category of those who feel entitled, smugly assuming that life owes them something for nothing, seems mistaken. Moral criticism needs to target the real offenders and not some generalized view of the "envious" or "whining" classes who want to take what others have without being willing to work for it themselves—or who simply want to deprive others of their hard-earned money out of spite. Assigning a label of "envy" to the wrong groups seems to create as significant a danger of "de-moralizing" the concept as using the label to sell cars and cosmetics or to brand computers and spa treatments: it keeps us looking in the wrong places, convincing us that other people are eating their hearts out, all the while we ignore the ways our own hearts are in need of careful examination.

Instead of tarring all the least advantaged with a "politics of envy" brush, some commentators have suggested that what our society really suffers from is a "politics of greed" on the part of the super rich.[12] But this does not seem to be an accurate analysis, either. Simply trading deadly sin epithets back and forth across the political aisle does little to advance the cause of communal understanding. The wealthy were not all born with silver spoons in their mouths that they now intend to keep clenched between their teeth, no matter what. The Forbes 400 list in 2014 began including a "self-made score," rating individuals on a scale from 1 (wealth completely inherited) to 10 (a total rags-to-riches story). According to this rating system, 69 percent of the wealthiest people in the United States created their own fortunes, pulling themselves upward through resourcefulness and dogged effort. Many such people have taken great risks, investing their energies in creating businesses and jobs, and subsequently dedicating significant amounts of their hard-earned income to philanthropy.[13] This is not greedy but generous. Still, it is misguided to assert that the earnings even of the self-made wealthy result from their efforts alone, entitling them to keep every penny. They have also benefited from structures paid for by the tax dollars of others: educational systems to prepare their workers; roads to get their goods to market;

patent laws to protect their inventions; police, fire departments, and military forces to keep them and their businesses secure. Indeed, some commentators argue it is not unreasonable to expect that those with the most to lose should pay the most to safeguard their possessions.

Land of Opportunity

In a closing assessment of envy and entitlement, it might help to return to an analogy made in passing several pages ago: the teacher who avoids playing favorites and attempts to treat all her students fairly. When students in her class work hard—reading not just the assigned material but more, spending hours studying for tests, preparing lab reports, or writing essays—surely they will be entitled to the high grades they receive. No teacher worthy of her gradebook would say to Stella Studious, "Granted, you earned a 100 on this test, but Fred only got a 50, so I'm going to take away 10 of your points (after all, you can afford to lose them and still have an A), and I'm going to give them to Fred to bring his mark up to passing." Fred Free-Rider, who never does any work—who simply shows up to class (and then, with a bad attitude), who does the bare minimum on assignments—is not entitled to a good grade just to keep peace in the classroom or prevent the teacher from being accused of discrimination by Fred's over-protective parents. If some outlandish points-from-Stella-to Fred strategy is the kind of redistribution that people like Bandow and Nozick have in mind when they speak of a politics of envy, no wonder they are disturbed by it.

But we can imagine another kind of classroom scenario. Stella, still our most gifted student, always finishes in-class assignments early. Is she, then, "entitled" to use the rest of her time playing computer games? After all, she "earned" that free time, too—or rather, she acquired it both because she worked efficiently and because the natural lottery blessed her with quick intelligence, through the luck of being born to smart parents. Or instead, may the teacher ask Stella to spend "her" time helping her classmates, freeing the teacher to work with another student? Laura, we'll call her, needs extra attention not because she is lazy but because she has a developmental reading disorder. The natural lottery also gifted Laura with intelligence, but in order to succeed in school, she needs special strategies and support. Where we come down on the "politics of envy" and the ethics of entitlement has a lot to do with whether we are picturing someone like Fred or someone like Laura as the intended beneficiary of our efforts.

In a self-proclaimed "land of opportunity," it is important that people like Laura not be overlooked. Opportunity, indeed, appears as a theme in an updated approach to Rawls published in 2013 by University of Pennsylvania professor Jeffrey Edward Green.[14] Green points out ways in which the growing gap between rich and poor threatens to undermine democracy by interfering with educational and political access. He reports on studies showing that young people born into privileged backgrounds have far greater prospects for wealth, education, and success than children *with equal talents and motivation* who are born into underprivileged backgrounds. Is this a state of affairs we would choose for our children from behind a "veil of ignorance"? Likewise, Green notes that without significant campaign finance reforms, people (and now, corporations) with wealth have far greater opportunity to exert political influence than the disadvantaged. To argue that such power rigs the game so that the rich keep getting richer while the poor have decreasing prospects of escaping from poverty sounds less like the grumbling of envy and more like a call to revitalize that "passion for equality" that Tocqueville found so admirable, but so hard to live up to, in the founding of our country.

Green is far from alone in voicing concerns about our growing national income gap. Research conducted independently in 2014 by Gallup polls and the Pew Research Center noted that two out of three Americans are now dissatisfied with the way income and wealth are distributed in the United States, and an even greater number identify the gap between rich and poor as a very big or moderately big problem facing the country.[15] As a result of this gap, social mobility—once the hallmark of a democratic rather than an aristocratic society—is shrinking. As the rungs on the ladder of success grow farther apart, scaling the ladder grows increasingly difficult. The United States now ranks lower in the potential for rags-to-riches success stories than Tocqueville's formerly class-bound France (or Germany, Sweden, Denmark, Spain, Canada, and Australia). Reflecting this newly sobering reality, the percentage of us who express satisfaction with the opportunity to "get ahead by working hard" has dropped from a high of 77 percent in 2002 to a just few points over 50 percent in 2014. If nearly half of our population no longer feels that efforts will be rewarded with success, we may indeed have created a fertile breeding ground for envy—along with resentment and indignation or, worse, simply resignation and despair. So we should ask ourselves seriously whether policies enacted to restore access and incentives would constitute a "politics of envy" or a politics of envy-preventing opportunity.

In his reflections about the young American democracy, Alexis de Tocqueville voiced a warning that some people's dreams for upward mobility would invariably be disappointed. As a consequence, he worried about the dangers of polis envy. Yet, he also noted, "The American legislators have succeeded to a certain extent in opposing the notion of rights to the feelings of envy."[16] That notion of envy-opposing rights includes the right to educational opportunities—even, or perhaps especially, for students like our hypothetical Laura who need specific support in order to succeed. It includes the right to a voice in government so as to have some say over policies that affect future chances of success. When, some two centuries after Tocqueville, these rights are being eroded—whether by the concentration of wealth and political influence in the hands of a few or by soaring higher education costs that severely limit the options of the less-advantaged—we have cause to be concerned.

Still, there is only so much that government-assured rights can do to address the problems of envy. Nozick is wise to have pointed this out. He reminds us that self-esteem both can and should be located in dimensions other than wealth. But, unfortunately, this means that status comparisons can be carried out in other dimensions as well. Thus, no one, regardless of social standing, is immune to feeling outclassed. Even billionaires may envy their business rivals' athletic prowess, their junior partners' romantic conquests, or their neighbors' exceptionally accomplished children.

Where, then, does this leave us? It takes us back to an old idea: that morality is, in the final analysis, not something we legislate, but something we cultivate. We teach it in our families, reinforce it in our schools, preach it in our places of worship, and work on it in the daily discipline of our own characters. But we must be clear: "morality" in this context means far more than "sexual morality," which it has come almost exclusively to connote in recent years. Rather, it means the full set of principles and practices by which we promote individual and communal flourishing. The regular practice of "virtues"—another good, old-fashioned word— offers the only sure path for rising above the envious tendencies in our status-conscious lives. Stories of moral exemplars in our concluding chapter help show us the way.

Chapter Seven

Redeeming Virtues

In the months leading up to the presidential election of 1860, William Henry Seward had every reason to think he would be the Republican nominee. He had already served two terms as governor of New York, then the most populous state in the country, and was completing his second term as a U.S. senator from that state. A politician in the best sense of the word, he was genuinely interested in the lives and concerns of his constituents. While some people may have objected to his programs—the expansion of public education, the creation of a vast infrastructure of canals and roadways for trade—they could still admire his principles. Even newspapers of the rival Democratic Party acknowledged that he was "beloved by all classes of people" and described him with adjectives like "frank," "reliable," "enterprising," "patriotic," and "dauntless."[1] Both Democratic and Republican publications confidently predicted his candidacy.

Seward could scarcely be faulted for taking such predictions seriously. Prior to the opening of the Republican convention, he drafted the speech with which he intended to resign from his senate seat to concentrate on the presidential race. In those days, it was considered unseemly for candidates to appear at the convention in person. So, while delegates in Chicago conducted their business, he hosted friends and family at his home in Auburn, New York, awaiting word of the vote. Meanwhile, crowds from all over the state gathered on the streets of Auburn with banners, flags, cannons, and champagne at the ready to salute the anticipated news.

At the start of the convention, Seward held a commanding lead. According to historian Doris Kearns Goodwin, many believe he would have won the nomination handily had balloting been conducted at the close of the second day. But the papers required for recording the tally had not yet been prepared, so the convention adjourned for the night—leaving twelve hours for opposition to Seward's candidacy to solidify.

Solidify, it did. Seward's electability was called into question, largely on the basis of his stance on abolition, which even many northern supporters thought was too radical. By the time the convention reopened on the morning of May 18, 1860, the tide had turned. After multiple ballots on which Seward lost more and more ground, Abraham Lincoln—presented as the moderate candidate—became the party's unanimous choice.

Seward's supporters were stunned. When news of the defeat arrived in the telegraph office back in New York, dazed and disappointed crowds slowly folded their celebratory banners and rolled the cannons off the town square. Seward himself must have been deeply disappointed. Yet, his public face never betrayed the slightest element of envy or resentment. Indeed, when the editor of the local newspaper could not find anyone willing to write about the newly formed presidential ticket, Seward did so himself. "No truer or firmer defenders of the Republican faith could have been found in the Union," he wrote, "than the distinguished and esteemed citizens on whom the honors of the nomination have fallen."[2]

Telling Tales, Again

In previous chapters, we have seen portrayals of envy used by moralists of earlier eras to warn their audiences away from this dangerous passion. Visual and verbal images alike accentuated its ugliness: the squinting eye, grasping hand, lips dripping with venom, and ravenous mouth devouring the sufferer's own heart. But the job of moral instruction does not stop with a pointing finger; it must also offer a beckoning hand. "Don'ts" need to be supplemented with "Dos," with suggestions of how we might turn away from destructive passions to lead more fully flourishing lives.

Seward's story provides a picture of such a life. To be sure, he would make no claims for his own sainthood, nor should we. In fact, months after the 1860 primary he remarked with wry humor that he was glad he did not keep a diary, since it would have borne witness to his wailing and gnashing of teeth upon first hearing the news of the convention vote. Still, for a public image of graciousness in defeat, he is exemplary. Within days after receiving word of a loss that might have embittered a lesser man, he pledged his support to the Lincoln/Hamlin ticket and bade his friends and former supporters follow suit. Not long after that, he embarked on the campaign trail on Lincoln's behalf and went on to become one of his closest friends in the "team of rivals" that Goodwin has made so famous.

What is it that enables people like Seward to endure a significant loss to a rival yet rise above any temptation to envy, while others stoop to malice under provocations that seem far less serious? In large part, this is a question of *character*, of the combination of traits and values that motivate our responses to morally significant situations. Simply put, someone of "good" character has developed the skills to exemplify the qualities her culture considers virtuous; someone of "bad" character fails to exercise these skills and may actually exercise contrary ones, pursuing what the culture considers to be vice.

Growing up in the first half of the nineteenth century, Seward would have experienced a character education that still counted envy among the vices, even if it was no longer necessarily considered one of seven "deadly sins." Schoolbooks like the *McGuffey Reader* or the *Character Building Reader* included numerous stories that warned young people against either envying or arousing envy in others. Advice manuals for parents recommended teaching children the violent brother-kills-brother story of Cain and Abel to drive home the serious consequences of envying.[3]

Of course, not everyone who came of age in Seward's day developed a noble, envy-free character; nor does everyone who grows up in the consumerist culture that has been expanding in the United States since the early decades of the twentieth century suffer the character warping of a constant focus on "me, me, me" and "more, more, more." Still, a nineteenth-century moral education understood, along with our medieval forebears, that we need tools to help us learn how to be and how not to be, and that stories, both exemplary and cautionary, are among the most effective implements in the toolbox.

Making Change

To use the tools provided by such stories, however, presupposes a belief that we truly can change the way we are. We are not stuck with a biological need to compete for status in order to improve our chances of reproducing, despite what the evolutionary psychologists tell us about envy's inevitability. We are not stuck with an innate temperament that makes us hyper-alert to perceived deprivations and eager to shore up our self-image by evening the score. Granted, as we learned from Harold Boris in chapter 5, some people do come into this world with more vulnerable dispositions than others or endure childhood experiences that incline them to defensiveness and fragile self-esteem. For such reasons, we should be careful about rushing to judgment. Since we cannot fully know the inner struggles of our neighbors, we would do better to spend our energies in self-examination, seeking ways that we can come closer ourselves to the ideal of a life well lived.

Although cultures disagree about the particulars of such a life, certain general features emerge.[4] These features come into even sharper relief if we narrow our focus to a specifically Christian image of human flourishing. That image expects us, among other things, to regulate our emotions: to shun envy, jealousy, contempt, and anger (at least of certain kinds and at certain provocations); to cultivate patience, gratitude, and kindness toward our neighbors. Thus, it will not do simply to say to the moralist, "I can't help myself; that's just the way I *feel*." While feelings of the sensation sort may be beyond our control, feelings of the emotion sort are not.

The difference goes something like this. Some feelings, as "sensations," are primarily physiological responses to stimuli. I smell supper cooking and, since I worked straight through lunch, I feel hungry and begin to salivate with expectation. Other feelings, as "emotions," involve significantly more than involuntary physiological responses; they also engage thoughtful evaluations of our circumstances. Suppose, for example, I am driving to work one morning and someone cuts in front of me on the highway, zooming off at speeds well above the posted limit. My initial reaction may be to feel angry. But what if I recognize the car as belonging to my junior colleague whose expectant wife's due date has recently passed, and I simultaneously realize that the highway leading to my workplace also leads to the hospital? Does my anger not transform into something quite different: hope, perhaps, or excitement, or anxiety about the couple's—and their baby's—safe arrival?

Literature discussing such questions about the philosophy, psychology, and morality of emotions has been accumulating over the past few decades. The perspective I find most helpful comes from Robert Roberts, who defines an emotion as "a way of 'seeing' things, when this seeing is grounded in a concern."[5] To apply his definition to my example: If I am not concerned about my safety or that of others on the highway or about basic driving courtesy, then I do not feel any emotion at all about the car that whips narrowly in front of mine. But if I *am* so concerned, then my subsequent emotional reaction to that provocation depends on the way I "see" the context of the person driving the speeding car.

Understanding emotions in this way suggests that I *can* help the way I feel, because I have a degree of control over the way I see things. This understanding harmonizes with teachings of the New Testament. Jesus warns us away from lust and anger, implying that we can be held accountable not just for our actions but also for our thoughts (Matt. 5:21–28). Paul advises us to cultivate the "fruit of the Spirit," many of which sound like emotions or their close kin: love, joy, peace, patience, and the like (Gal. 5:22). He tells us to "Rejoice" and a few verses later, gives us clues as to how to do this, by directing our attention—or in Roberts's language, construing our circumstances—in positive ways: "Finally, beloved," he writes, "whatever is true, whatever is honorable, whatever is just, whatever is pure, whatever is pleasing, whatever is commendable, if there is any excellence and if there is anything worthy of praise, think about these things" (Phil. 4:4, 8).

Whether coming to us from Paul, medieval moralists, or more contemporary thinkers, virtue theory holds that we can make change in our lives by working to see situations that evoke emotional responses in more constructive ways. Specifically with regard to envy, this means practicing new ways of looking not just at our relationships with our rivals but also at our relationships with ourselves, with our material context, and with our ultimate context—which is to say, with God. But before illustrating each of these new ways of seeing, we must understand why changing our orientation to envy matters so profoundly.

Redeeming "Sin"

As we noted in our opening chapter, except in a few specific contexts, it has become both uncommon and unpopular in our day to speak of envy as a sin. A recent book on the psychology of envy even argues that the label is counterproductive. According to this argument, the religious taboo implicit in the word prevents us from recognizing envy as a normal and natural emotion; as a result, we are likely to bury our feelings under layers of shame when we would be better served by exposing them to the light of therapeutic intervention.[6] While it certainly seems right that owning up to envy is better for us in the long run than hiding and denying it, to insist that envy is "only natural" misses an important moral point. Perhaps there are natural impulses of our hearts of which we *should* feel ashamed, impulses that distort our relationships whether we ever act on them or not, impulses that demean our own dignity as human beings and as children of God. Perhaps what we need is a better way of understanding the label "sin" rather than an elimination of the label altogether.

In *Speaking Christian*, theologian and best-selling author Marcus Borg offers such a way. He points out that the word "sin," like a number of other key terms in the Christian vocabulary, has lost much of its meaning of late and needs to be reinterpreted for current use.[7] In the popular imagination, he notes, "sin" is most readily associated with hellfire-and-damnation preaching: sinners must repent of wrongdoings before it is too late, before a just and righteous God condemns us to a life of eternal punishment. But, Borg insists, the biblical view of sin is far richer than this. Sin does not just refer to individual bad acts but to a power that holds us captive, to an obsessive focus on ourselves, promoted and reinforced by the social structures in which we live. To say that human beings are sinners is, therefore, not simply to voice an accusation of guilt; more fully, it is to acknowledge a need for healing and transformation—a transformation not just in our individual lives but in our world as well.

Envy needs such healing and transformation because it distorts and diminishes our living. Most obviously, it damages our own spirits, causing us to eat our hearts out, as the old images so aptly put it, poisoning our thoughts and gnawing away at our peace of mind. Instead of people of noble character able to rise above challenges with grace and equanimity (think again of William Henry Seward), we become petty grousers. Fixating on the pain of our injured egos, we worry perpetually about how we are being treated and how well we measure up.

Even if we never do anything overtly about it (committing, say, acts of vandalism or character assassination), envy damages our relationships with our neighbors as well. When we view other people through the squinted eye of the envious gaze, we narrow them down to a single dimension: instead of richly rounded individuals with lives full of joys and sorrows, gifts and challenges of their own, we see them exclusively as the unfair possessors of privileges we crave but do not have. Instead of fellow children of God, we make them out to be enemies whose downfall we secretly (or not so secretly) desire.

Particularly in its contemporary consumerist form, envy further distorts our relationship to our material context, to the creation. One environmental ethicist, Louke van Wensveen, has interpreted this quite literally: thinking the grass to be greener on the other side of the fence, some people make aggressive use of herbicides and fertilizers on their own side, with toxic results. Less literally, our constant striving to keep up with the Joneses contributes to an economy of waste that is rapidly depleting the earth's resources. "The old vice of envy regains moral significance in the midst of an environmental crisis," van Wensveen warns.[8]

In the dim reaches of our evolutionary past, certain forms of acquisitive competition may have contributed to our struggle for survival. But in our own context, envy that fuels and is fueled by competitive consumerism is simply no longer sustainable.

As an environmental ethicist writing for a secular audience, van Wensveen uses the word "vice" rather than "sin" in speaking of envy. In the tradition of the seven deadlies, the two terms appeared fairly interchangeably; theologians warned against "principal vices" or "capital sins." But this tradition always assumed the existence of God as the One who created us in such a way that some practices (like patience, kindness, love, hope: the "virtues") contributed to our flourishing, whereas others (like pride, envy, anger, sloth: the "vices") kept us and our communities from thriving. Secular virtue ethics no longer makes this assumption; instead, it traces the roots of flourishing/non-flourishing to general features of human nature or specific cultural norms. Still, this branch of ethics has done much in recent decades to redeem the term "vice" from its own connotations of moralistic finger-wagging, whereby the vice squad of a police force is the one focused restrictively on behaviors related to sex, drugs, and alcohol. Thanks to virtue ethicists, we can now label other serious abuses of nature (environmental degradation) or of human nature (greed, arrogance, apathy) as "vicious."

Still, in a Christian context, any such abuses are not only against nature and human nature but also against their Author. Envy, thus, is not just demeaning to our own dignity, disruptive of our personal relationships, and destructive of our relationship to the natural world. Most gravely of all, it distorts our relationship with God. To envy the status of another person flies in the face of the Christian claim that each of us is a unique and beloved creation; it betrays ingratitude toward the One who gave us the gift of life in the present and promises us life in eternity. Envy turns us away from ultimate goods to make idols of temporary and trivial ones, the trappings of status and success; it measures our worth on too small a scale, assuming our value to lie in our finite possessions or accomplishments rather than in God's infinite mercy and love. Insofar as we are called to love God with *all* our heart, soul, mind and strength, envy is failure to live up to the first and greatest commandment.

But the good news is this: if envy is "sin," then we are not left on our own to solve the problem. After all, we do not redeem our own sin; that is done for us. Insofar as sin is "a power that holds us captive" (recall Borg's reclaimed definition), God's work of salvation has already set us free. The more fully we realize the depth of that liberating love, the more we can live out of it as the wellspring of our attitudes and actions instead of attempting to prove our worth through desperate, competitive posturing. Grace empowers us to cultivate practices that demonstrate our freedom from the bondage of self-absorption and to correct the vicious thoughts and behaviors that grow out of our sinful state.

A first such practice is repentance, another word Borg wants to redeem for contemporary use. The biblical view, he points out, involves much more than begging for forgiveness for our misdeeds. In the New Testament, to repent means "to go beyond the mind we have"—the mind that is socialized by our personal and cultural upbringing—in order that we might come to "see things in a new way."[9] What better language could there be to describe the process of living a life freed from envy, since envy exemplifies "the mind we have," socialized by a competitive and consumerist culture? We need to "go beyond" this mind, to look again at ourselves, our neighbors, our relationship to the creation and the Creator, seeing them all in a new light.

Seeing Ourselves: Humility

Bertie Pollock is a lovable six-year-old with a well-intentioned but markedly overbearing mother, Irene. The two of them figure in the 44 Scotland Street series by Edinburgh author Alexander McCall Smith (best known for his No. 1 Ladies' Detective Agency novels). Intent on Bertie's edification, Irene overschedules him with yoga classes, saxophone lessons, Italian *conversazione*, Kleinian psychotherapy, and play dates with an equally overbearing six-year-old girl named Olive. Poor Bertie just longs to have a friend of his own and to do normal boy things: be a Cub Scout, own a penknife, go camping.

One day, at the end of a series of adventures and misadventures, Bertie ends up at a house where another six-year-old boy happens to live. Andrew invites Bertie to his room to show him the treasures it contains. One of these—wonder of wonders!—is a penknife. Bertie examines it raptly and points out the word *Italia* inscribed on the blade, noting that this means it was made in Italy. "You speak Italian?" Andy asks. Bertie acknowledges that he does. Andy responds, "You must be jolly clever, Bertie. . . . I only speak English."[10]

It is easy to overlook a scene like this, in fiction or in real life. On the surface, it is just a passing conversation between two small boys in the process of forging a friendship. Yet, while there is nothing showy or heroic about Andy's exclamation, it demonstrates something important about his character. He is blessed with an assurance about himself that enables him to take pleasure in someone else's accomplishment without the need to downplay it or assert a countering talent of his own ("You speak Italian? That's a dumb language"; "You speak Italian? Well, I can ride a unicycle!").

As if this were not enough demonstration of Andy's good character, a few lines later he takes a Swiss Army penknife from his bedside table and offers it to Bertie. "I want you to have it," Andy says. "You're my friend, you see. So I want you to have it." Bertie is deeply touched by this generosity. We should be, too. After all, such moments are the stuff of the quieter virtues, and pausing to savor them helps us cultivate our own moral repertoire.

Granted, both admiration and generosity—the traits Andy shows toward Bertie—are virtues that illustrate ways of seeing and responding to a neighbor. But even more fundamentally, such attitudes emerge out of a way of seeing the self. This is a way of seeing that has escaped from the posturing of an ego intent on its own status and possessions and is instead characterized by humility.

Humility can be mistaken for things it is not: false modesty, for example, or low self-esteem. But true humility does not consist in pretending we are less talented than we are or in having a low opinion of ourselves. As Robert Roberts points out, the opposite of humility is not healthy self-esteem but rather "pushiness, scorn of 'inferiors,' rejoicing in the downfall of others, envy, resentment and grudge-bearing, ruthless ambition, haughtiness, shame at failure or disadvantageous comparison, and the need to excel others so as to think well of oneself."[11] It is no wonder that envy and pride are so closely linked in the vice trees of the cardinal sins tradition, a tradition well aware of how multiple vicious tendencies stem from a common root and grow entangled with one another.

In the deadly sins tradition, to be sure, humility was most often counseled as the virtue contrary to pride. But linking humility with envy is not unprecedented. In a letter to a friend, the fourth-century monk Evagrius, originator of the capital vices schema, wrote that one who "loves esteem" is prone to envy and should rather strive to "become like the one who humbled himself," presenting himself to all as a servant.[12] Viewed in the light of Roberts's analysis, this connection between envy and self-humbling makes sense. Modern-day psychologists confirm Evagrius's observation that the most intense envy is often found in pathological narcissists: those who love the esteem of others, those whose inflated self-concept demands frequent feeding.[13] Even the non-pathological among us can recognize that when we persistently evaluate situations with an eye to how we compare with our neighbors, we are betraying an unhealthy preoccupation with our own egos. The "way of seeing" that runs counter to envy consists of a self-understanding that is less narcissistic, less inflated, more down-to-earth (the root of the word "humility" is *humus*)—an ability to acknowledge both our gifts and flaws without needing to prove ourselves better than anyone else in order to bolster our self-image.

Such humility is not the same thing, though, as complacency. After all, there are things we should want to change about ourselves, whether our own failures at loving God and neighbor or the failures of our world at embodying justice and peace. Nor is it the same thing as resignation, though some historical preaching against envy as a sin has surely fostered such confusion. Moralists in earlier eras occasionally argued that each person had a divinely appointed place in a hierarchical social order and that seeking after the privileges of a higher station amounted to rejecting God's plan. But we have seen in previous chapters that neither longing nor emulation is the same thing as envy: *longing* wishes for a good but does not begrudge it to those who already have it; *emulation* seeks to imitate rather than belittle a good's possessors. Moreover, if the distribution of goods is unfair, resistance to such unfairness is more properly called *indignation* than *envy*. Striving to improve rather than resign ourselves to our lot in life does not therefore mean we are lacking in humility.

The key is whether in the midst of our striving we are able to live at peace. The envious person is never satisfied: no matter what she acquires or accomplishes, someone else will always manage more. The chronic malcontent of envy eats our hearts out, leaving a hole in our center that can never be filled. Our best hope is to plug the hole with the humble conviction that our worth ultimately does not come from our own achievements but from grace.

Seeing Our Neighbors: Benevolence

Mma Grace Makutsi (another character from the fertile moral imagination of Alexander McCall Smith) has never had much luck with men.[14] She is smart and hardworking—so much so that she earned 97 percent on her final examination from the Botswana Secretarial College, a fact she can manage to work into almost any conversation. But she is not pretty. She has an "unfortunate complexion" and wears extremely large glasses. She has always feared that the desirable romantic relationships are destined for more conventionally attractive women: women like Violet

Sephotho, another graduate from her class at the Secretarial College, but one who achieved a far less distinguished examination result.

In a desperate attempt to find a suitor, Mma Makutsi enrolls in a dancing class. To her dismay, the only man who seeks her out as a partner is the painfully shy Phuti Radiputhi. His stammer is so severe that he can barely communicate, on the dance floor or off. His feet never seem to go in the right directions or keep time to the right beat. Meanwhile, as luck would have it, Violet Sephotho has enrolled in the same class and inevitably managed to attract the most desirable partner, a man who guides her gracefully and elegantly across the floor.

But Violet cannot rest content with this good fortune; she has to rub it in the face of her school-day rival. By chance, she and Mma Makutsi run into each other in the ladies' room at the dance hall. Violet begins by sarcastically "complimenting" Mma Makutsi's "courage" in wearing her prized green shoes, sneering: "I would be frightened that people would laugh at me if I wore shoes like that." She goes on from this to attack the less attractive woman's dance partner: "That man through there. Is that your uncle or something?"

Mma Makutsi knows Violet is trying to provoke her. Before responding, she pauses to ponder what her mentor, Mma Ramotswe (the worldly wise head of the No. 1 Ladies' Detective Agency), might advise saying under the circumstances and comes up with this reply. "The man you are dancing with is very handsome," Mma Makutsi observes. "You are lucky to have such a handsome man to dance with. But then you are a very pretty lady, Mma, and you deserve these handsome men. It is quite right that way."[15] Violet Sephotho is nonplussed. Unable to provoke the envy she had wanted, she stalks away. Mma Makutsi has answered pettiness with benevolence and, in so doing, scored a moral victory—not so much over Violet as over herself.

"Benevolence" is an umbrella term for an array of generous-spirited attitudes that help us see our neighbors in an envy-countering light. When we are concerned for the well-being of others, we stand ready to give of ourselves in ways beyond the expected: offering the benefit of the doubt, forgiving or overlooking slights and offenses, striving in all circumstances to be respectful and caring. Material giving forms part of such benevolence as well: cheerful, ungrudging acts that share our goods (whether in the form of desired dance partners or desired penknives) with others. Many of the "fruits of the Spirit" named by Paul fall under this general heading: love, patience, kindness, generosity, gentleness, and in some instances (like Mma Makutsi's) self-control.

As we have already seen in our chapter of "arresting images," a number of generous-spirited, benevolent virtues were counseled in the deadly sins tradition as ways of countering envy. Giotto's fresco of *Invidia* in the Scrovegni Chapel depicts a hag who clutches at a moneybag with one hand while reaching sideways with the claw-like fingers of the other to grasp at a neighbor's goods. The fresco opposite is *Karitas*—the embodiment of love or charity—who holds a brimming bowl of fruit in one hand while reaching upward with the other to offer a piece to Christ. Peter Bruegel's engraving of Envy depicts woman eating her own heart out, surrounded by vignettes of dogs fighting over bones and people fighting over shoes; the contrasting image is Love, a woman surrounded by scenes of merciful acts (feeding the hungry, visiting the sick, and so on) while she herself offers her heart to a child.

Love and charity likewise figure in the earliest pastoral advice given in the deadly sins tradition for dealing with envy. Gregory the Great, we will recall, is the theologian who first added envy to the list of capital vices when he modified inventories of "eight demonic thoughts" inherited from Evagrius and Cassian two centuries earlier. In his book of *Pastoral Care*, he names "the kindly" as those people demonstrating the most direct contrast to "the envious." In his *Source Book of Self-Discipline*, he offers counsel to the latter that sounds much like the Golden Rule: if we guard against doing to others what we would not want done to ourselves, then we will keep ourselves from ill will and hurtful speech; if we focus instead on doing for others what we would like done for us, we will seek ways to "return good things for evil and better things for good."[16]

The advice is simple enough; the trick is following it. As with so many of the behavioral virtues, a constructive first step in practicing benevolence is to act "as if." Perhaps we do not initially feel kindly disposed to the colleague who has just beaten us out of a desirable promotion (or dance partner). We can still muster the self-control, like Mma Makutsi, to offer words of congratulation and squelch disdainful comments we might be tempted to make behind the person's back. We can even attempt public praise for the rival's abilities (recall Seward's editorial following his loss to Lincoln in the Chicago primary) and pray publicly or privately, offering thanks for the ways such a person's gifts enrich us and our communities. This is not a counsel of hypocrisy. Rather, it is an acknowledgment that our behavior is shaped by the thoughts we think and the words we speak. Kindness is not merely a matter of an inherently rosy temperament; it can be cultivated through deliberate action. Sometimes words of admiration do spring easily to our lips ("You must be jolly clever, Bertie"), but sometimes they must be hard-won ("You are a very pretty lady, Mma, and you deserve these handsome men"). Either way, they form part of the repertoire of benevolence toward those we see as more fortunate than ourselves.

But benevolence also extends to those less fortunate. In these instances, it is more likely to take the shape of compassion and empathy, born of training ourselves to experience the neighbor's adversity as touching our own well-being: not just as something that *could* someday happen to us, but as something that *does* diminish us as members of a common family. Such compassion directly counters envy's evil twin, Schadenfreude, the malicious glee that rejoices in a rival's downfall. But it also prevents envy proper from taking root. When we work to see all our neighbors as vulnerable and cherished children of God, like ourselves, we become more fully able both to rejoice with those who rejoice and to weep with those who weep.

It is worth recalling that both Old and New Testaments connect envy with an image of the Evil Eye (*ra ayin* in Hebrew, *ophthalmos poneros* in Greek). Envious people look on their rivals with a narrowed and withering gaze—although as we have seen (most graphically in Giotto's depiction), any intended harm actually turns back onto the enviers themselves. Aptly enough, in Hebrew Scripture a contrast term to envy is the "Good Eye" (*'ayin tovah*, sometimes loosely translated as "generosity"): the eye wide open to perceive God's blessings in the neighbor and respond to that person with an equally open heart.[17] Envy prevention involves learning to see with the "Good Eye," seeing "beyond the mind we have," looking on the neighbor through God's eyes rather than our own.

Seeing Our Material Context: Simplicity

Oseola McCarty was born in 1908 in Mississippi and was raised by her grandmother, a widow and the daughter of a slave. From her grandmother, Oseola learned the value of hard work, whether it was scratching out a living on a seven-acre farm or taking in laundry to supplement the family income. As a child, she wanted to become a nurse, but she had to drop out of school in the sixth grade to care for a sick relative and keep the family laundry business going.

For seventy-five years, Oseola did washing and ironing for other people until arthritis in her fingers made it impossible for her to continue. She never owned a car, but once a week she would push a cart to and from the grocery store nearly a mile away; on Sundays, she would walk two miles to church. She owned a radio and a small black-and-white television set, but she never bought other luxuries: just food, clothing, and utilities. After making a regular offering to her church, she put the rest of her weekly earnings, meager as they were, into the bank.

By the time she was eighty-six years old, she had saved the staggering sum of $250,000. She decided to give it all away: 10 percent to her church, 30 percent to her relatives, and the remaining 60 percent to a scholarship fund she endowed at the University of Southern Mississippi, so that other people could get the education that she was never able to pursue.[18]

Oseola's story exemplifies virtues we have already discussed, both humility and benevolence. Like Bertie's friend, Andy, she is at peace with who she *is* and thereby happy to give what she *has* to others. But beyond these character traits related to ways of seeing herself and seeing her neighbors, Oseola also demonstrates virtues related to ways of seeing her material circumstances. These "material virtues" go by a number of different names, including thrift, temperance, and frugality.

Each name carries its own connotations. Thrift was a popular virtue in schoolbooks like the *McGuffey Reader* and still calls up images of the Boy and Girl Scout laws dating from the early 1900s ("a Scout is thrifty"). "Temperance" has a far longer history in Western moral traditions, figuring since Plato as one of four cardinal or foundational virtues (along with prudence, justice, and fortitude). However, because the Prohibition era in the United States succeeded in connecting the word so strongly to a refusal of alcohol, some contemporary ethicists find it less useful for talking about the need for restraint in our broader habits of spending and consuming. "Frugality," once a key virtue both of Roman Catholic monastic traditions and the Protestant work ethic, fell into disfavor in the early twentieth century, when economists, sociologists, and journalists began to argue that desires should be fulfilled rather than restrained. In that context, "frugal" came to imply a penny-pinching and even anti-progress orientation. For this reason, environmental theologian James Nash calls frugality a "subversive virtue," all the while insisting on its renewed significance for our era. In an age of ecological crisis, frugality assists us not only in living within our personal means but also within planetary means, which we can no longer pretend are inexhaustible.[19]

Thrift, temperance, and frugality can all be usefully contained under the single heading, "simplicity." Environmental ethicists Joshua Gambrel and Philip Cafaro define simplicity as "a conscientious and restrained attitude toward material goods."[20] People who practice simplicity, like Oseola McCarty, make careful decisions about what and how much they consume, aware that the quality of life does not depend on the quantity of possessions. But a lifestyle of voluntary simplicity does not confine itself to saying no to excess, waste, and needless luxury; it also says yes to the pursuit of fulfillment through meaningful activities and relationships rather than things. Simplicity is a way of living that is fruitful (frugal), thriving (thrifty), and well-tempered (temperance), focused not simply on our own well-being but also that of other people and other species, for the present and for generations to come.

Of course, it is possible to reorient the way we see our material context and still be victims of envy, since status comparisons have to do not only with possessions but also with attainments of other kinds. Still, an essay in the most recent collection of theory and research on envy maintains that the pairing of a global consumer culture with urban anonymity (whereby we know little about our neighbors beyond those status markers we can actually *see*) means that consumer goods have become the "chief source of envy" today, more than "traits, abilities, power, privilege, freedom, and fun."[21] Whether or not this claim is correct, deliberate efforts at simplifying our lives can help loosen the grip we have on stuff—or the grip it has on us—in ways that free us to find joy in values that are not zero sum, in arenas in which our neighbors' having more does not necessitate our having less.

Moreover, simplicity, like any of the other envy-countering virtues, should not be considered in isolation. Oseola McCarty did not practice a frugal lifestyle for the sake of frugality; to do so, indeed, would have run the risk of turning the virtue of simplicity into the vice of stinginess. Rather, she practiced it for the sake of having more to give away. Simplicity thus joins forces with benevolence, even as benevolence is made possible by such humble contentment with ourselves that we can willingly offer goods or services or the sheer gift of admiration to others: "You must be jolly clever, Bertie"; "You are a very pretty lady, Mma, and you deserve these handsome men"; "No truer or firmer defenders of the Republican faith could have been found in the Union than the distinguished and esteemed citizens on whom the honors of the nomination have fallen."

In short, no single virtue but rather a combination of virtues is required to correct the vice of envy. A negative image for such combination might be a broad-spectrum pesticide equipped to handle a wide range of destructive organisms. Insofar as envy involves elements of pride, malice, and greed (analogous to roundworms, mites, and ticks), it must be attacked on multiple fronts at once. A more positive image would be that of companion planting. When marigolds and basil are cultivated in the same plot as tomatoes, not only do the tomatoes taste better, but also white flies and aphids are kept naturally at bay. When we simultaneously practice humility, benevolence, and simplicity, the result is more "flavorful" and flourishing lives for ourselves, our communities, and our planet.

Indeed, such flourishing is why environmental ethicists call simplicity a "virtue" and not simply a lifestyle option. Virtues, by definition, are traits that help promote individual and collective well-being, whereas vices are character traits that result in harm. By such definitions, the materialist values of our culture constitute vices, insofar as they damage our psychological, spiritual, and even physical health. Lottery winners, for example, have been shown to end up less happy than they were before their windfall victories; patterns of overconsumption generate debt, a chronic dissatisfaction that undermines relationships, and a host of stress-related illnesses.[22] On a broader scale, conspicuous consumption puts a strain on planetary resources, resulting in pollution, climate destabilization, the loss of species, and widening gaps between wealthy and poor. To "go beyond the mind we have" in viewing our material context thus requires a radical transformation of our cultural as well as personal values.

More clearly than any of the other revisions we must make in order to live freed from envy, re-visioning our material context illustrates what Marcus Borg noted about sin. Not just personal wrongdoing, sin is "a power that holds us captive" through an obsessive self-focus reinforced by the social structures in which we live. Such structures include, for example, an advertising industry whose job is to stimulate personal dissatisfaction and promote envy in order to fuel a constantly growing economy. As long as we are convinced this is the only way an economy can function, we will likely remain victims to a vicious treadmill. Stepping off will require the combined efforts of ethicists, economists, and environmentalists to assist in reshaping our norms.[23] In the meantime, though, we can learn from people like Oseola McCarty to act in "subversive," countercultural ways.

Seeing Our Ultimate Context: Gratitude

Morrie Schwartz was dying. Diagnosed with ALS, Lou Gehrig's disease, the former Brandeis University sociology professor decided to approach his final months as one last classroom. What lessons about living might be learned and taught by someone willing to confront his own dying head-on? As Morrie grappled with such questions, his "students" came to number in the millions. Ted Koppel recorded some of his wisdom in a series of *Nightline* interviews. Mitch Albom captured still more in a best-selling book, eventually made into a movie, *Tuesdays with Morrie*.[24]

Raised in a Jewish family, Morrie (who always preferred to be called by his first name) became agnostic in midlife. In his final months, however, he found himself embracing a broad-based spirituality infused with elements of Judaism, Christianity, Buddhism, and other religions. He meditated regularly. He acknowledged having conversations with God, although he also confessed he was not sure this was the best name for the all-encompassing, sacred reality in which we all live and into which we all return.

Over and over, Morrie spoke to his interviewers about the importance of remaining *aware*: aware of feelings, whether pleasant or painful; aware of family and friends, both near and far; aware of our surroundings. He did not sugarcoat the difficulties of his illness, but he did not succumb to them, either. "I give myself a good cry if I need it," he admitted. "But then I concentrate on all the good things still in my life." "It's horrible to watch my body slowly wilt away to nothing. But it's also wonderful because of all the time I get to say good-bye." Gesturing toward a sun-filled window, he remarked: "I look out that window every day. I notice the change in the trees, how strong the wind is blowing. It's as if I can see time actually passing through that windowpane. Because I know my time is almost done, I am drawn to nature like I'm seeing it for the first time."

Even the indignities of the physical dependency forced on him by his loss of motor control became occasions for appreciative awareness. Having once feared the time when he would no longer be able to attend to his own toileting needs, when that day came he discovered he could let go of culturally engrained embarrassment and find pleasure in the experience: "The strangest thing. . . . Now I enjoy when they turn me over on my side and rub cream on my behind so I don't get sores. . . . I revel in it. I close my eyes and soak it up."

Living in each moment in this way, bathing his own pain in the same gentle compassion he extended to all who wrote and spoke to him about the suffering in their lives, he found he had no more need to make comparisons. When envy came to him, envy for those who could still dance or swim or do other things beyond his capabilities, he said simply, "I feel it, and then I let it go." While recognizing that it might be impossible for the old not to experience twinges of envy regarding the young, he went on to advise: "The issue is to accept who you are and revel in that." When we "do the kinds of things that come from the heart," he suggested, we will no longer have to be "dissatisfied" or "envious" or "longing for somebody else's things." On the contrary, we will be overwhelmed by the unique gifts of our own lives.

Like Oseola McCarty, Morrie Schwartz exemplifies multiple virtues: humble contentment, even in the most challenging circumstances; benevolent giving, even when he might understandably have conserved all his time and strength to care for himself; simplicity of life, focused more on cultivating relationships than acquiring things. But it is for a fourth set of virtuous dispositions that he becomes our guide for the closing pages of this chapter. These virtues do not simply affect the ways we view ourselves, our neighbors, or our material context. Rather, they orient us to our ultimate context, to transcendent sources of meaning, value, and purpose. While these virtues go by various names—attunement, appreciation, elevation—we will sum them up under the heading of gratitude.

Clearly, Morrie Schwartz practiced attunement to his surroundings. Indeed, he cultivated awareness not just of pleasant realities but also of painful ones. Deeply in touch with his own feelings, with his family and ever-widening circle of "students," with the realm of nature visible outside his window and the realm of spirit entered through his meditations, he demonstrated the character trait of appreciation: a facility for recognizing and enjoying excellence wherever it might appear. In their book *Character Strengths and Virtues*, psychologists Christopher Peterson and Martin Seligman label appreciation a "virtue of transcendence" because "it connects those who possess it to something larger than themselves, whether it is beautiful art or music; skilled athletic performance; the majesty of nature; or the moral brilliance of other people."[25] By practicing appreciation, we honor things for what they are in themselves without needing to relate them to our personal agendas. Likewise, in appreciation we are not required to *do* anything except be present in the moment, letting ourselves be filled with wonder and awe.

As with other virtues in our companion planting, the connection between appreciation and envy can be indirect as well as direct. Occasionally we are called to appreciate our immediate rivals in order to counter our competitive inclinations—as we saw in William Henry Seward's appraisal of the Lincoln/Hamlin presidential ticket. But more broadly, appreciating *anything* can serve as an envy preventive. When we focus our gaze on aesthetic beauty or moral excellence, we enlarge our spirits in such a way that the pettiness of envy feels out of place, like a dirty gym sock left lying in the middle of a room we have just spring cleaned.

Psychologist Jonathan Haidt reserves the word "elevation" for the type of appreciation we feel in response to moral excellence.[26] Morrie's story is elevating. Depending on a reader's sensitivities, the other stories in this chapter might prove so as well. According to Haidt's research, such stories make us feel a distinctive warmth and expansiveness in the chest along with a desire to become better people ourselves. Such responses suggest further reasons to use "telling tales" in moral instruction: they not only offer examples of how to improve our lives but inspire us to take up the challenge.

Appreciation and elevation thus focus our vision on aspects of our context that move us "beyond the mind we have," beyond inclinations to bitterness and dissatisfaction, so that we instead see beauty and excellence around us. But such recognition frequently calls us to a further response: a desire to offer thanks to whatever source we understand as ultimately responsible for such experiences. Gratitude inclines us to see goodness neither as random happening nor as personal accomplishment but as *gift*.

Not just a matter of perfunctory politeness, gratitude is a *virtue* that promotes personal and communal flourishing. Melanie Klein, one of the first psychologists to give envy a central place in her analysis of the human condition, named gratitude as its direct counter, enabling us to appreciate goodness in ourselves and others and thus develop in healthy directions.[27] Ann and Barry Ulanov, whose Jungian exploration of *Cinderella and Her Sisters* we explored in chapter 5, suggest that the healing of envy consists in becoming an "ardent appreciator" of the good, taking gladly and gratefully what is given.[28] More recently, psychologist Robert Emmons and his colleagues have done extensive research demonstrating that habitually grateful people experience fewer symptoms of physical illness, greater optimism, and richer overall life satisfaction. When we take more appreciative notice of our experiences, we feel stronger empathy toward others and forge stronger social bonds. Emmons concludes: "Gratitude takes us outside ourselves" to see our lives "as part of a larger, intricate network of sustaining relationships." He thus repeatedly refers to it as a "firewall of protection against envy."[29]

Ingratitude, on the other hand, correlates with anxiety, depression, resentment, materialism, and loneliness. Ungrateful people see little need to give thanks; feeling entitled to everything that comes their way, they are either too jaded to take delight in goodness or too proud to acknowledge any debt to the generosity of others—or more significantly, of an ultimate Other. Thus, in the Protestant tradition of Christianity, ingratitude is not simply a vice but a deep manifestation of sin. Martin

Luther calls it the "first level of perdition," maintaining that Lucifer fell on account of ingratitude toward the Creator; John Calvin ascribes the fall of Adam and Eve to infidelity and ingratitude, hankering after more than was allotted to them and thus showing contempt for the gifts God had already given.[30]

In contrast, thankfulness figures as a central part of faithful and flourishing lives. The imperative to give thanks appears over and over in the Old and New Testaments, and Emmons's research shows that people who attend religious services and engage in religious activities may indeed practice what they preach in this regard: they demonstrate more gratitude than others, a stronger inclination to share their belongings, and a lesser inclination to envy.[31] Beyond greater statistical frequency, Christian gratitude further manifests a distinctive shape that Robert Roberts explains in this way: The Christian who firmly trusts in the presence and promises of God lives in a "cosmic" context in which gratitude is always apt, even though in specific "local" context it may seem unwarranted.[32] Thus, Paul is able quite reasonably to insist that the recipients of his letters should give thanks not only on obviously happy occasions but "in all circumstances" (1 Thess. 5:18).

Living Large

Psychologists and theologians thus agree that global gratitude is good for our individual and communal health. They further argue that we can train ourselves in this virtue, effectively spreading a thick layer of spiritual mulch to prevent weeds of envy from sprouting and choking our spirits or our communities. Robert Emmons, for example, recommends keeping a gratitude journal, a daily record of matters large and small for which we are thankful. Melanie Klein commends the practice of grace before meals as a way of freeing ourselves from resentment and envy. Paul exhorts us to "rejoice always" and "pray without ceasing" (1 Thess. 5:16–17). Multiple religious traditions, in fact, recommend that we punctuate our days, from waking to sleeping, with prayerful appreciation of the blessings we have received.

In concluding, then, we would do well to pause and consider a number of the envy-preventing blessings for which we might regularly express our gratitude. We might, for example, be grateful for our rivals, whose excellence pushes us to be better than we would otherwise be, the way a fast runner ups the speed of everyone in the pack. We might appreciate the gifts these rivals offer and the work they do that takes a burden away from us (even if it is a burden we once thought we craved). We might be grateful for neediness that undermines our impulses to self-sufficiency, showing us how we live—as Peterson and Seligman stated and as Morrie Schwartz confirmed—within complex networks of care. We might be grateful for those people who help us in our times of sorrow or give us the opportunity to help them in theirs. We might be grateful to be children of God, loved as deeply as we could ever hope to be loved, showered with a spiritual abundance that does not diminish but rather multiplies by being shared.

In all these things, we are more than blessed. Why, then, would we envy? As Marcus Borg pointed out earlier in this chapter, repentance looses us from the bondage of sinful self-absorption, enabling us "to go beyond the mind we have" so that we come to "see things in a new way." In this new way of seeing, we discover our eagerness to break free of the petty anxieties, insecurities, and rivalries that hold us captive, emerging instead into magnanimous lives. Paul calls us to the task, in words movingly translated by Eugene Peterson:

> Dear, dear Corinthians, I can't tell you how much I long for you to enter this wide-open, spacious life. We didn't fence you in. The smallness you feel comes from within you. Your lives aren't small, but you're living them in a small way. I'm speaking as plainly as I can and with great affection. Open up your lives. Live openly and expansively! (2 Cor. 6:11–13 *The Message*)

Paul's desire for us, like the desire of the artists and moralists of the deadly sins tradition, is that we practice *living large*: large not in the magnitude of our possessions or accomplishments but in our openness to one another and to grace. As we have seen repeatedly, the envious heart is small: constricted and self-devouring, empty and hurting, yet too infatuated with its torment to let it go. In vibrant contrast, the magnanimous heart—characterized by humility, benevolence, simplicity, and gratitude—continually expands in the delight of giving itself away. The benefits of such living—to ourselves, our neighbors, and even our planet—encourage us to expose our secret sin to the fresh air of healing.

Notes

Introduction

1. This point was most famously made by Robert Burton, *The Anatomy of Melancholy*, part I, section 2, member 3, subsection 7 (1638). (Project Gutenberg, 2004), Kindle edition.
2. Jane Ciabattari, "Will the '90s Be the Age of Envy?" *Psychology Today* (December 1989): 46–50.
3. Rebecca Konyndyk DeYoung, *Glittering Vices: A New Look at the Seven Deadly Sins and Their Remedies* (Grand Rapids: Brazos Press, 2009), 41.
4. Robert Solomon, ed., *Wicked Pleasures: Meditations on the Seven Deadly Sins* (New York: Rowman and Littlefield, 2000); Dan Savage, *Skipping towards Gomorrah: The Seven Deadly Sins and the Pursuit of Happiness in America* (New York: Dutton, 2002). DeYoung's work, cited above, offers a notable counterpoint to these cavalier analyses.
5. Dorothy Sayers, "The Other Six Deadly Sins," in *Creed or Chaos?* (New York: Harcourt, Brace, 1949), 63–85.

Chapter 1: Envy Appeal

1. In addition to newspaper accounts at the time of the events, the story received documentary treatment in "Texas Cheerleader Murder Plot," *American Justice*, first broadcast October 22, 1997, by Arts and Entertainment Network. ABC produced a made-for-television movie, *Wanting to Kill: The Texas Cheerleader Story* in 1992, and HBO, *The Positively True Adventures of the Alleged Texas Cheerleader-Murdering Mom* in 1993.
2. James D. Norris, *Advertising and the Transformation of American Society, 1865–1920* (New York: Greenwood Press, 1990), 26.
3. Thorstein Veblen, *The Theory of the Leisure Class: An Economic Study of Institutions* (New York: MacMillan Company, 1912), 68.
4. William and Mary Morris, *Dictionary of Word and Phrase Origins*, vol. 1 (New York: Harper and Row, 1962), 202.
5. Susan J. Matt, *Keeping Up with the Joneses: Envy in American Consumer Society, 1890–1930* (Philadelphia: University of Pennsylvania Press, 2003).

6. Theodore McManus's copy for Cadillac ad, reprinted from *Saturday Evening Post*, quoted in Norris, *Advertising and the Transformation*, 154.

7. Allen B. DuMont Laboratories, item ID TV0100 in the Ad*Access collection of the John W. Hartman Center for Sales, Advertising, and Marketing History at Duke University.

8. Laurence Shames, *The Hunger for More: Searching for Values in an Age of Greed* (New York: Times Books, 1989), 123.

9. *Autoweek*, March 10, 1997, 13.

10. Gregory Solman, "Y&R Brands Ties Jaguar to 7 Deadly Sins," *Adweek* (September 13, 2004), accessed October 17, 2014, http://www.adweek.com/news/advertising/yr -brands-ties-jaguar-7-deadly-sins-74788.

11. Eric Peters, "2001 Jaguar XK8," *The Car Connection*, last modified February 26, 2001, http://www.thecarconnection.com/review/1002333_2001-jaguar-xk8.

12. Brenda Boyd Raney and Melissa Elkins, "Verizon Wireless and LG Launch the Envy of All Mobile Phones—The enV by LG," verizonwireless.com, November 26, 2006, http://www.verizonwireless.com/news/article/2006/11/pr2006-11-27a.html.

13. Chris Matyszczyk, "Why AT&T's Next iPhone Ad Is the Greatest Ever iPhone Ad," CNET.com, November 12, 2013, http://www.cnet.com/news/why-at-ts-next-iphone -ad-is-the-greatest-ever-iphone-ad/.

14. For the original fragrance launch, see *Harper's Bazaar* (June 1998): 71. For the updated version targeted toward a younger audience, see "Envy Me Gucci for Women," Fragrantica.com, accessed February 11, 2015, http://www.fragrantica.com/perfume /Gucci/Envy-Me-682.html.

15. "About Envy," envymedical.com, last modified 2012, http://www.envymedical.com /index.php?option=com_content&view=article&id=63&Itemid=79&lang=en; Massage Envy Spas, accessed October 12, 2014, http://www.massageenvy.com.

16. Christopher Lasch, *The Culture of Narcissism* (New York: W. W. Norton, 1978), 73.

17. Richard W. Pollay, "The Distorted Mirror: Reflections on the Unintended Consequences of Advertising," *Journal of Marketing* 50 (April 1986): 28.

18. Richard Fox and T. J. Jackson Lears, eds., introduction to *The Culture of Consumption: Critical Essays in American History 1880–1980* (New York: Pantheon Books, 1983), xi.

19. Philip Rieff, *The Triumph of the Therapeutic: Uses of Faith after Freud* (New York: Harper and Row, 1966).

20. See, for example, T. J. Jackson Lears, *No Place of Grace: Antimodernism and the Transformation of American Culture 1880–1920* (Chicago: University of Chicago Press, 1994).

21. Fosdick's *Adventurous Religion* quoted in T. J. Jackson Lears, "From Salvation to Self-Realization: Advertising and the Therapeutic Roots of the Consumer Culture, 1880–1930," in *The Culture of Consumption*, 14.

22. Lears, *No Place of Grace*, 13.

23. Robert Coles, "The Hidden Power of Envy," *Harper's Magazine* (August 1995): 20–23.

24. Julie Taylor, "Envy: Is it Hurting or (Surprise) Helping You?" *Cosmopolitan* 224, no. 3 (March 1998): 158.

25. For just a few examples, see articles like the following: Rebecca Johnson, "I'm Happy for You. Really. How to Deal with Success When It's Somebody Else's," *Mademoiselle* 99, no. 8 (August 1993): 134; and Barbara Lang Stern, "Your Well-Being (Envy's Destructive Effect)," *Vogue* 177, no. 11 (November 1987): 450.

26. "Age Cannot Wither Them: Why Envy Is the Reason the Elderly Are Seeking Youth," *Economist* 346, no. 8064 (April 16, 1998): 30; Kate White, "I Want What She's Got," *Working Mother* 21, no. 9 (September 1998): 10; and "Gadget Envy," *Business Journal* 16, no. 2 (October 9, 1998): 21.

27. Alice Walton, "Jealous of Your Facebook Friends? Why Social Media Makes Us Bitter," *Forbes* (January 22, 2013), accessed February 11, 2015, http://www.forbes.com/sites /alicegwalton/2013/01/22/jealous-of-your-facebook-friends-why-social-media-makes -us-bitter/; Alex Williams, "The Agony of Instagram," *New York Times* (December 13, 2013), accessed October 21, 2014, http://www.nytimes.com/2013/12/15/fashion /instagram.html.

28. Geneen Roth, *Feeding the Hungry Heart: The Experience of Compulsive Eating* (Indianapolis: Bobbs-Merrill, 1982), 13.

Chapter 2: Rival Definitions

1. Morton Bloomfield, *The Seven Deadly Sins* (Lansing: Michigan State College Press, 1952), 59.

2. Gore Vidal, quoted in *The Sunday Times Magazine*, London (September 16, 1973).

3. See Rabbi Nilton Bonder, *The Kabbalah of Envy: Transforming Hatred, Anger, and Other Negative Emotions*, trans. Julia Michaels (Boston: Shambhala Publications, 1997); and George R. A. Aquaro, *Death by Envy: The Evil Eye and Envy in the Christian Tradition* (Lincoln, NE: iUniverse, Inc., 2004).

4. Joseph Berke suggests this interpretation of "mud in the eye" in *The Tyranny of Malice: Exploring the Dark Side of Character and Culture* (New York: Summit Books, 1988), 53.

5. Antisthenes, quoted in Gonzalo Fernández de la Mora, *Egalitarian Envy: The Political Foundations of Social Justice*, trans. Antonio de Nicolás (New York: Paragon House, 1987), 6.

6. Hans Weiditz, "Envy," reprinted in Wilhelm Fraenger, *Hieronymus Bosch* (New York: Dorset Press, 1989), 49.

7. On the relationship between envy and proximity, see Helmut Schoeck, *Envy: A Theory of Social Behavior*, trans. Michael Glenny, Betty Ross (Indianapolis: Liberty Fund, 1987), 26.

8. Aristotle, *Rhetoric*, Book II, 1387b-1388b, trans. W. Rhys Roberts (Oxford: Clarendon Press, 1946).

9. Thomas Aquinas, *Summa Theologica* IaIIae, q. 28, a. 4.

10. John Rawls, *A Theory of Justice* (Cambridge, MA: The Belknap Press of Harvard University Press, 1971), 533.

11. Aristotle, *Rhetoric*, Book II, 1386b.

12. Aristotle, *Nicomachean Ethics* II.vii.15, trans. H. Rackham (Cambridge, MA: Harvard University Press, 1926).

13. Max Scheler, *Ressentiment*, trans. Lewis Coser and William Holdheim (Milwaukee, WI: Marquette University Press, 1994). See also Friedrich Nietzsche, *On the Genealogy of Morals*, trans. Walter Kaufmann and R. J. Hollingdale (New York: Vintage Books, 1967).

14. George Crabb, "Jealousy," in *Crabb's English Synonymes* (New York: Grosset & Dunlap, 1938?), 463–64.

15. Gordon Clanton and Lynn Smith, eds., *Jealousy* (Englewood Cliffs, NJ: Prentice-Hall, 1977), vi.

16. Schoeck, *Envy*, 25. Subsequent quotes in this paragraph are from Schoeck, 135–37.

17. Jen Pilla, "Home Envy Killer Gets Life after Jury Deadlocks," *Charlotte Observer* (July 3, 1998).
18. Nancy Friday, *The Power of Beauty* (New York: HarperCollins, 1996), 86.

Chapter 3: Arresting Images

1. Georges Duby, *The Age of the Cathedrals: Art and Society 980–1420*, trans. Eleanor Levieux and Barbara Thompson (Chicago: University of Chicago Press, 1981), 231–32.
2. "Hugh of St. Victor on Virtues and Vices," with a translation of the original text (*De quinque septenis seu septenariis*) by Joachim Wach, *Anglican Theological Review* 31 (1949), 25–33.
3. See Ernest William Tristram, *English Wall Painting of the 14th Century* (London: Routledge and Kegan Paul, 1955), 85.
4. Jennifer O'Reilly, *Studies in the Iconography of the Virtues and Vices in the Middle Ages* (New York: Garland Publishing, 1988), 375.
5. Adolf Katzenellenbogen, *Allegories of the Virtues and Vices in Mediaeval Art from Early Christian Times to the Thirteenth Century*, trans. A. J. P. Crick (New York: W. W. Norton, 1964), figures 64 and 65, described on 65–67.
6. Described by Emile Mâle in *The Gothic Image; Religious Art in France of the Thirteenth Century*, trans. Dora Nussey (New York: Harper, 1958), 107–8.
7. M. D. Anderson, *Drama and Imagery in English Medieval Churches* (Cambridge: Cambridge University Press, 1963), 8–10.
8. Dante, *Inferno*, Canto XVII, lines 43–78. The senior Scrovegni is not identified by name but by the familial insignia of "a fat and azure swine" emblazoned on a white purse that he wears slung about his neck.
9. For further details about the artistic program of the Scrovegni Chapel, see James Stubblebine, ed., *Giotto: The Arena Chapel Frescoes* (New York: W. W. Norton, 1969).
10. For full discussion of the work, see Mia Cinotti, *The Complete Paintings of Bosch* (New York: Harry N. Abrams, 1969); and Wilhelm Fraenger, *Hieronymus Bosch*, trans. Helen Sebba (New York: Dorset Press, 1989).
11. Bruegel signed his own name multiple ways, but for the last ten years of his life consistently used this spelling. See H. Arthur Klein, *Graphic Worlds of Peter Bruegel the Elder* (New York: Dover Publications, 1963), vii. This book contains reproductions and commentaries on the whole series of deadly sin engravings. Envy is treated on 106–7.
12. For interpretation of this series, see Kathleen Wilson-Chevalier, "Sebastian Brant: The Key to Understanding Luca Penni's *Justice and the Seven Deadly Sins*," *Art Bulletin* 78, no. 2 (June 1998): 236–63.
13. Sebastian Brant, *The Ship of Fools*, trans. Edwin H. Zeydel (New York: Dover, 1962), 185.
14. Ibid.
15. Morton Bloomfield, *The Seven Deadly Sins* (Lansing, MI: Michigan State College Press, 1952), 243.
16. Hilary B. Price, 1998, distributed by King Features Syndicate, Inc.

Chapter 4: Telling Tales

1. Lloyd W. Daly, "The Book of Xanthus the Philosopher and Aesop His Slave" or "The Career of Aesop," in *Aesop without Morals* (New York: Thomas Yoseloff, 1961), 31–90. For the various fables below, see also *Caxton's Aesop*, ed. R. T. Lenaghan (Cambridge, MA: Harvard University Press, 1967).

2. The legend involving St. Martin is found in Eugene Mason, *Aucassin & Nicolette and Other Mediaeval Romances and Legends* (New York: E. P. Dutton & Co., 1919), 129–30; the allusion to *The Ways of the Righteous* is in Solomon Schimmel, *The Seven Deadly Sins: Jewish, Christian, and Classical Reflections on Human Psychology* (New York: Oxford University Press, 1997), 60–61.

3. Quoted in G. R. Owst, *Literature and Pulpit in Medieval England*, 2nd rev. ed. (New York: Barnes and Noble, 1961), 180.

4. Aeschylus, *The Oresteia*, trans. Richard Lattimore (Chicago: University of Chicago Press, 1953). All further line references are from this translation, unless otherwise noted.

5. Aeschylus, *The Oresteian Trilogy*, trans. Philip Vellacott (Baltimore: Penguin Books, 1956). Lattimore renders this passage as, "Do not cross my path with jealousy by strewing the ground with robes." The Greek word in question is *epiphthonon*.

6. Plutarch, *Cyropedia* 1.4.15, quoted in Peter Walcot, *Envy and the Greeks: A Study of Human Behaviour* (Warminster, England: Aris and Phillips, 1978), 17.

7. Plutarch, *Moralia* 91A, quoted in Walcot, *Envy and the Greek*, 20.

8. Ovid, *Metamorphoses*, trans. A. E. Watts (San Francisco: North Point Press, 1980), 46.

9. See Mary E. O'Carroll, *A Thirteenth Century Preacher's Handbook: Studies in MS Laud Misc. 511* (Toronto: Pontifical Institute of Mediaeval Studies, 1997), 25.

10. Geoffrey Chaucer, "The Pardoner's Prologue," in *Canterbury Tales*, trans. Nevill Coghill (New York: Penguin Books, 2003), 244.

11. "The Parson's Prologue," in *Canterbury Tales*, 485–86.

12. "The Parson's Tale," in *Canterbury Tales*, trans. J. U. Nicolson, in *Chaucer*, vol. 22 of Great Books of the Western World (Chicago: Encyclopedia Britannica, 1989), 516–17.

13. Guillaume de Deguileville, *The Pilgrimage of Human Life*, trans. Eugene Clasby (New York: Garland Publishing, 1992). Subsequent quotes from this translation can be found on 112–17.

14. John D. Sinclair's commentary on Canto XIV, *Purgatorio* (New York: Oxford University Press, 1972), 194.

15. Dante quoted by Mark Musa in the introduction to his translation of *Inferno* (New York: Penguin Books, 1984), 42.

16. William Langland, *Piers Plowman*, The C Version, Passus VI, trans. George Economou (Philadelphia: University of Pennsylvania Press, 1996).

17. The following account of the pageant of the sins comes from Edmund Spenser, *The Faerie Queene*, book I, canto 4, modernized and edited by Douglas Brooks-Davies (Rutland, VT: J. M. Dent, 1996), 50–61.

18. Christopher Marlowe, *Doctor Faustus*, II.ii., ed. Sylvan Barnet (New York: New American Library, 1969), 50.

Chapter 5: Spoiled Psyches

1. Bruno Bettelheim, *The Uses of Enchantment* (New York: Vintage Books, 1977).

2. In a pop psychology work on envy, Betsy Cohen refers to the practice of "lying low" as *The Snow White Syndrome* (New York: Macmillan, 1986).

3. Helmut Schoeck, *Envy: A Theory of Social Behavior* (Indianapolis: Liberty Press, 1966), 55.

4. Mark Gillman, *Envy as a Retarding Force in Science* (Brookfield, VT: Avebury, 1996).

5. Schoeck, *Envy*, 56. Also George M. Foster, "The Anatomy of Envy: A Study in Symbolic Behavior," *Current Anthropology* 13, no. 2 (April 1972): 172.

6. Adrian van Kaam, *Envy and Originality* (Garden City, NY: Doubleday, 1972), 42.
7. See Bettelheim, *Uses of Enchantment*, 236; and Sheldon Cashdan, *The Witch Must Die: How Fairy Tales Shape Our Lives* (New York: Basic Books, 1999), 88.
8. Bettelheim, *Uses of Enchantment*, 265.
9. Ann and Barry Ulanov, *Cinderella and Her Sisters: The Envied and the Envying* (Philadelphia: Westminster Press, 1983).
10. Melanie Klein, *Envy and Gratitude and Other Works 1946–1963* (New York: The Free Press, 1975), 180–88, 195–96.
11. Harold Boris, *Envy* (Northvale, NJ: Jason Aronson, 1994), 23.
12. Joseph Berke, *The Tyranny of Malice: Exploring the Dark Side of Character and Culture* (New York: Summit Books, 1988), 88.
13. Terence Kealey, "Destination Hell" (a series on the seven deadly sins), *New Scientist* (March 28, 1998): 26.
14. Sara Hill and David Buss, "The Evolutionary Psychology of Envy," in *Envy: Theory and Research*, ed. Richard Smith (New York: Oxford University Press, 2008), 60–72.
15. Robert Wright, *The Moral Animal: Why We Are the Way We Are: The New Science of Evolutionary Psychology* (New York: Vintage Books, 1994), 26.
16. Kealey, "Destination Hell," 27.
17. Jerome Neu, "Jealous Thoughts," in *Explaining Emotions*, ed. Amélie Oksenberg Rorty (Berkeley: University of California Press, 1980), 439–40.
18. Alfie Kohn, *No Contest: The Case against Competition*, rev. ed. (Boston: Houghton Mifflin, 1992), 11.
19. Ibid., 37.
20. Thomas H. Huxley, *Evolution and Ethics* (London: Macmillan & Co., 1894), 49–50.
21. Wright, *Moral Animal*, 257.

Chapter 6: Polis Envy

1. Biographical details are from Leo Damrosch, *Tocqueville's Discovery of America* (New York: Farrar, Straus, and Giroux, 2010).
2. Laurence Shames, *The Hunger for More: Searching for Values in an Age of Greed* (New York: Times Books, 1989), 47.
3. Alexis de Tocqueville, *Democracy in America*, trans. Henry Reeve (Hazleton, PA: The Electronic Classics Series, 2002-2013), 224, accessed February 18, 2015, http://www2.hn.psu.edu/faculty/jmanis/tocqueville/dem-in-america1.pdf.
4. Ibid., 702.
5. Plutarch, quoted in Peter Walcot, *Envy and the Greeks: A Study of Human Behaviour* (Westminster, England: Aris & Phillips, 1978), 55–58.
6. Doug Bandow, *The Politics of Envy: Statism as Theology* (New Brunswick, NJ: Transaction Publishers, 1994), 301–3.
7. Matt Lauer interview with Mitt Romney, *The Today Show*, accessed February 18, 2015, http://www.today.com/video/today/45955255#45955255.
8. Josh Gressel, *Embracing Envy: Finding the Spiritual Treasure in Our Most Shameful Emotion* (Lanham, MD: University Press of America, 2014), 48.
9. John Rawls, *A Theory of Justice* (Cambridge, MA: The Belknap Press of Harvard University Press, 1971).
10. Ibid., 533.

11. Robert Nozick, *Anarchy, State, and Utopia* (New York: Basic Books, 1974).

12. See, for example, Susan Milligan, "Mitt Romney and 'Envy' vs. 'Greed,'" *U.S. News & World Report* (January 12, 2012), accessed February 18, 2015, http://www.usnews.com/opinion/blogs/susan-milligan/2012/01/12/mitt-romney-and-envy-versus-greed.

13. Agustino Fontevecchia, "The New Forbes 400 Self-Made Score: From Silver Spooners to Bootstrappers," *Forbes* (October 2, 2014), accessed February 18, 2015, http://www.forbes.com/sites/afontevecchia/2014/10/02/the-new-forbes-400-self-made-score-from-silver-spooners-to-boostrappers/.

14. Jeffrey Edward Green, "Rawls and the Forgotten Figure of the Most Advantaged: In Defense of Reasonable Envy toward the Superrich," *American Political Science Review*, 107, no. 1 (February 2013): 123–38.

15. Rebecca Riffkin, "In US, 67% Dissatisfied with Income, Wealth Distribution," Gallup (January 20, 2014), accessed February 18, 2015, http://www.gallup.com/poll/166904/dissatisfied-income-wealth-distribution.aspx; and Richard Wike, "With 41% of Global Wealth in the Hands of Less Than 1%, Elites and Citizens Agree Inequality Is a Top Priority," Pew Research Center (November 8, 2014), accessed February 18, 2015, http://www.pewresearch.org/fact-tank/2014/11/08/with-41-of-global-wealth-in-the-hands-of-less-than-1-elites-and-citizens-agree-inequality-is-a-top-priority/.

16. Tocqueville, *Democracy*, 357.

Chapter 7: Redeeming Virtues

1. Details in this and the following biographical paragraphs are drawn from Doris Kearns Goodwin, *Team of Rivals: The Political Genius of Abraham Lincoln* (New York: Simon and Schuster, 2005). Quotes from the *New York Herald* are on 12–13.

2. William Henry Seward in the *Auburn Daily Advertiser*, quoted in Goodwin, *Teams of Rivals*, 251.

3. Susan Matt, *Keeping Up with the Joneses: Envy in American Consumer Society, 1890–1930* (Philadelphia: University of Pennsylvania Press, 2003), especially 162–69.

4. Christopher Peterson and Martin Seligman have compiled an intriguing list of character strengths they hold to be common across cultures and historical eras. See *Character Strengths and Virtues: A Handbook and Classification* (New York: Oxford University Press, 2004).

5. Robert C. Roberts, *Spirituality and Human Emotion* (Grand Rapids: Eerdmans, 1982), 16. This preliminary exploration has been considerably expanded in the author's more recent *Spiritual Emotions: A Psychology of Christian Virtues* (Grand Rapids: Eerdmans, 2007).

6. Leyla Navaro and Sharan Schwartzberg, eds., *Envy, Competition, and Gender* (New York: Routledge, 2007), 205.

7. Marcus Borg, *Speaking Christian: Why Christian Words Have Lost Their Meaning and Power—And How They Can Be Restored* (New York: HarperCollins, 2011), 2.

8. Louke van Wensveen, *Dirty Virtues: The Emergence of Ecological Virtue Ethics* (New York: Humanity Books, 2000), 99. Other environmental ethicists focus more on greed. See, for example, Philip Cafaro, "Gluttony, Arrogance, Greed, and Apathy: An Exploration of Environmental Vice," in Ronald Sandler and Philip Cafaro, eds., *Environmental Virtue Ethics* (Lanham, MD: Rowman and Littlefield, 2005), 135–58.

9. Borg, *Speaking Christian*, 158–59.

10. Alexander McCall Smith, *The Importance of Being Seven* (New York: Anchor Books, 2012), 280.

11. Roberts, *Spirituality and Human Emotion*, 62.

12. Evagrius Ponticus, "Letter to Eulogios," trans. Robert E. Sinkewicz in *Evagrius of Pontus: The Greek Ascetic Corpus* (New York: Oxford University Press, 2003), 31.

13. See, for example, Otto Kernberg, *Borderline Conditions and Pathological Narcissism* (Northvale, NJ: Jason Aronson, 1975), 227–29, 233.

14. Alexander McCall Smith, *In the Company of Cheerful Ladies* (New York: Pantheon Books, 2004).

15. Ibid., 126.

16. Gregory the Great, *Pastoral Care*, trans. Henry Davis (Westminster, MD: Newman Press, 1950), 113–14; and Peter of Waltham, *Source Book of Self-Discipline: A Synthesis of Moralia in Job by Gregory the Great*, trans. Joseph Gildea (New York: Peter Lang, 1991), 245–46.

17. George R. A. Aquaro, *Death by Envy: The Evil Eye and Envy in the Christian Tradition* (Lincoln, NE: iUniverse, Inc., 2004), 28–31.

18. Rick Bragg, "All She Has, $150,000, Is Going to a University," *New York Times* (August 13, 1995), accessed October 19, 2014, http://www.nytimes.com/1995/08/13/us/all-she-has-150000-is-going-to-a-university.html.

19. James Nash, "On the Subversive Virtue: Frugality," in *Ethics of Consumption: The Good Life, Justice, and Global Stewardship*, ed. David Crocker and Toby Linden (New York: Rowman and Littlefield, 1998), 427.

20. Joshua Gambrel and Philip Cafaro, "The Virtue of Simplicity," *Journal of Agricultural and Environmental Ethics* 23 (2010): 87.

21. Russell Belk, "Marketing and Envy," in *Envy: Theory and Research*, ed. Richard Smith (New York: Oxford University Press, 2008), 211.

22. Gambrel and Cafaro, "Virtue," 96; and Julie Juola Exline, "Antidotes to Envy: A Conceptual Framework," in *Envy: Theory and Research*, 319.

23. A full bibliography of "must-read" books discussing alternative models can be found at the website for CASSE, Center for the Advancement of the Steady State Economy, http://steadystate.org/discover/reading-list/.

24. The information and quotations below are drawn from Mitch Albom, *Tuesdays with Morrie: An Old Man, a Young Man, and Life's Greatest Lesson* (New York: Doubleday, 1997), 81–82, 163, 57, 84, 116, 119–20, 128.

25. Peterson and Seligman, *Character Strengths*, 520.

26. Jonathan Haidt, "Elevation and the Positive Psychology of Morality," in *Flourishing: Positive Psychology and the Life Well-Lived*, ed. C. Keyes and J. Haidt (Washington, DC: American Psychological Association, 2003). Peterson and Seligman coin the term *Tugendfreude* to indicate emotions that find joy in the talents, skills, and virtues of others—a play on the word *Schadenfreude*, meaning joy in a neighbor's misfortune. See *Character Strengths and Virtues*, 545.

27. Melanie Klein, *Envy and Gratitude and Other Works 1946–1963* (New York: The Free Press, 1975), 188.

28. Barry and Ann Ulanov, *Cinderella and Her Sisters: The Envied and the Envying* (Philadelphia: Westminster Press, 1983), 158 and 123.

29. Robert A. Emmons, *Thanks! How Practicing Gratitude Can Make You Happier* (Boston: Houghton Mifflin, 2007), 11, 186, 54, 10, and 43.

30. See the analysis of Luther's Commentary on Romans in Jairzinho Lopes Pereira, *Augustine of Hippo and Martin Luther on Original Sin and Justification of the Sinner* (Göttingen: Vadenhoeck & Ruprecht, 2013), 413–14. John Calvin, *Institutes of the Christian Religion*, 2.1.4, ed. John T. McNeill, trans. Ford Lewis Battles, LCC (Philadelphia: Westminster Press, 1960), 245.

31. Emmons, *Thanks!*, 95.

32. Robert Roberts, "Emotions among the Virtues of the Christian Life," *The Journal of Religious Ethics* 20, no. 1 (Spring 1992): 44.

Index

CPSIA information can be obtained
at www.ICGtesting.com
Printed in the USA
LVOW04s2114210316
480154LV00006B/8/P

9 780664 259709